IT'S NOT
YOUR
MONEY

ALSO BY
TOSHA SILVER

Change Me Prayers: The Hidden Power of Spiritual Surrender

Outrageous Openness: Letting the Divine Take the Lead

Make Me Your Own: Poems to the Divine Beloved

IT'S NOT YOUR MONEY

HOW TO LIVE FULLY FROM
DIVINE ABUNDANCE

TOSHA SILVER

HAY HOUSE, INC.

Carlsbad, California • New York City
London • Sydney • New Delhi

Published in the United States by: Hay House, Inc.: www.hayhouse.com® • *Published in Australia by:* Hay House Australia Pty. Ltd.: www.hayhouse .com.au • *Published in the United Kingdom by:* Hay House UK, Ltd.: www .hayhouse.co.uk • *Published in India by:* Hay House Publishers India: www .hayhouse.co.in

Cover design: Micah Kandros • *Interior design:* Nick C. Welch

Library of Congress has cataloged the earlier edition as follows:

Names: Silver, Tosha, author.
Title: It's not your money : how to live fully from divine abundance / Tosha
  Silver.
Description: 1st Edition. | Carlsbad, CA : Hay House Inc., 2019.
Identifiers: LCCN 2018049662 | ISBN 9781401954734 (hardback)
Subjects: LCSH: Finance, Personal--Religious aspects. | Money--Religious
  aspects. | Spiritual life. | BISAC: BODY, MIND & SPIRIT / Inspiration &
  Personal Growth. | BODY, MIND & SPIRIT / Mysticism. | SELF-HELP / Personal
  Growth / Success.
Classification: LCC HG179 .S47457 2019 | DDC 332.024--dc23 LC record available
at https://lccn.loc.gov/2018049662

Tradepaper ISBN: 978-1-4019-5475-8
E-book ISBN: 978-1-4019-5474-1

14 13 12 11 10 9 8 7 6 5
1st edition, February 2019
2nd edition, September 2020

Printed in the United States of America

To Maha Kali

CONTENTS

Ironically

when you let the Divine take the lead

old desires often begin to hatch

and be fulfilled

anyway

(as a gift from Love Herself)

except now

you're not

their slave

— Tosha Silver, "Unshackled," *Make Me Your Own*

INTRODUCTION

Dad, I TOLD you. If God's not included,
I just get bored.

— Little girl in line at Kohl's

If anyone told me years ago that I'd be writing a spiritual book about money, I'd never have believed it. But when I look back on my life, it makes total sense. All my other books have centered on the practical ways to surrender and let the Divine lead, and money might be the single stickiest topic for this approach. Many spiritually-minded people will invite the Divine into almost anything, except the moolah.

I grew up the middle child in a middle-class Jewish family where my parents worked incredibly hard for my two brothers and me to feel physically comfortable. I'll be grateful to them forever. Nonetheless, my obsession from a very young age was a single topic: Impending Doom. No matter how seemingly safe we were, I was always sure that in some vague and intractable way, disaster waited right around the next corner.

Perhaps this incessant fear came from being born just a couple of generations from the Holocaust with distant relatives who'd perished there. As a kid, I'd heard stories about pogroms, concentration camps, and collapsing economies. Perhaps terror was encoded straight into my DNA.

Or maybe it was the legacy of past lives replete with suffering, loss, and travail. All I know is that despite growing up in a quiet ranch-style home with a weeping willow tree I madly loved in the backyard, nonstop anxiety was my steady reality. My constant wait for that indefinable other shoe to drop emerged in some wild and dramatic ways.

When I was six, my mom left the house one rainy afternoon without saying anything, which was rare. Within twenty minutes, I was running down the street, banging on doors and frantically screaming her name, sure she'd been kidnapped. When I found her calmly sitting in a neighbor's kitchen, drinking coffee and borrowing eggs, I collapsed into her lap in heaving tears of relief. She gave the neighbor a wry look like, "Yes, here is my darling, hypersensitive daughter."

When my parents went out for an occasional date, my older brother would look forward to winning Scrabble with Patti, our babysitter. Meanwhile, I'd sit with my face flush against the cold bedroom window, staring down the dark street, waiting hour after hour for the lights of their returning Pontiac. When I'd finally hear the key in the door, joy would flood my body like sunshine at midnight. I'd feel as if tragedy had somehow once again been averted for another evening. But who knew when it might strike next?

So yes, I had a feverish imagination with a sense of nonstop peril, though I learned early to appear as brave and normal as possible. Once I graduated from college, those survival fears immediately swamped me, almost in spite of the job opportunities that came. I began teaching ESL part-time at a community college and eventually had a side business doing bodywork and intuitive counseling.

The terror of "not-enough" was a constant storm cloud. If a client canceled, I panicked. Though I covered the bills month to month, I kept fretting about what I'd do if I *couldn't* one day. This led to such overwork and exhaustion that by the time I was 30, I was bedridden for 3 years with adrenal failure, something I wrote about in my first two books.

By the '90s, when I was regaining my health, the New Age ideas about manifesting and the Law of Attraction were beginning to boom. Many of my clients were enamored with the notion that *any* desire could be "magnetically attracted" through visualizations and positive thoughts. They put up vision boards with pictures of everything they wanted, from Balinese vacations to artist's lofts in Manhattan. But I also noticed that many lived in fear that any negative thought might stunt the delivery. Some even blamed themselves ferociously when each and every wish didn't hatch, assuming they'd surely "blocked" them.

Yet right from the start, this Grand Chase of the Wishes, kind of like a metaphysical Iditarod, left me feeling empty and bemused. Growing up in relative comfort yet beset by constant fear, I had no illusions that fixating on that laundry list of desires could ever bring much peace. I'd watched some of my own clients create fame and fortune, then have it all crash. People manifested soul mates, then lost them just as fast. One painful desire only seemed to beget another.

At the same time, I longed to go deeper into my own spiritual studies of yogic philosophy. I'd been introduced to yoga in college and I sensed it held many answers, far beyond stress reduction and a better butt. (Not that there's anything wrong with that, as Seinfeld would say.) I knew there had to be a deeper, more nuanced answer to life than to be born, chase stuff, and die. I longed to find a sense of safety and enoughness—the sense that despite ups and downs, crashes and cataclysms, one could some-how prosper—separate from life's inevitable flux.

So I began to study famous ancient texts from India such as the Bhagavad Gita and Patanjali's *Yoga Sutras*. I found unspeakable comfort in their ideas such as detachment (*vairagya*), nongrasping (*aparigraha*), and surrender (*ishvara pranidhana*). They were the delicious, calming drinks that my fevered mind had been thirsting for forever.

At the same time, I discovered the works of Florence Scovel Shinn, a metaphysical author from the last century. She'd been a no-nonsense New Yorker who most notably wrote *The Game of Life and How to Play It*. Through Flo, I "got" that God is the Source of all. Period. The End. I came to see that this Source could be invoked in all situations, no matter how seemingly impossible. Florence's under-standing of Divine Order—that a coherent plan underlay even the biggest challenges—began to feed my starving psyche. Combined with my studies of yogic texts, a new way forward began to emerge from the blinding fog of my fears.

It was as if God just rolled over laughing: "You know, honey, you're here to learn how to *serve* Me, not issue one command after another. So, just let Me take over. You'll stop living in abject terror and recall why you were born. All needs will be met beyond what you can imagine!"

Besides, my own ego could never manifest much of anything even when it tried! And while I knew that the Law of Attraction had some truth (our thoughts *in part* indeed create our reality), I came to see that other laws reliably operated as well. From the yogic texts, I was espe-cially drawn to the Law of Prarabdha Karma, the idea that in each lifetime, a soul is born for a distinct *curriculum*.

Every desire might *not* be meant to occur, no matter how many vision boards you make.

I began to sense that the peace I'd always craved would come from learning to live in conscious harmony with this Force. I ferociously longed to learn how to let *It* use me, rather than trying to use It to get wishes. The hyper-vigilant chasing of desires felt like utter micromanagement to me. So many people thought, *If I'm on guard every blessed second, maybe I'll finally, finally get what I want.* But I was coming to see that the ego could be a bottomless pit of wishes, not all of which are for the soul's highest good.

Through Florence Scovel Shinn's vision of Divine Source—the idea that no person, place, or thing was my protection and safety, only Love Itself—my life began to shift even more. I learned how to drop the ego's agenda and let go, sometimes very, very painfully. But as I did this, a new sense of holy abundance began to emerge. It had *nothing* to do with manifesting millions and everything to do with knowing how to open, give, receive, and serve the Flow.

This is something I believe anyone can learn, regardless of age, race, nationality, gender, sexual orientation, or anything else. Because in the most practical way, God transcends all of it.

Now, I'm in no way ignoring the very real "isms" that afflict and infect this society, often in the most brutal and unjust ways. Nonetheless, when you invite and embody this Source, your current, temporary incarnational body and conditions are transcended. You open to *however* Divine largesse is meant to come for you personally. With willingness, curiosity, or even just "Hell, I'm completely exhausted," this new way can be learned.

ℭHE ORIGINAL COURSE

The idea for this book originated from an online class I taught a couple years ago—one people had begged me to do forever. Many had read my other books or had been part of a Living "Outrageous Openness" online forum I run, where the art of letting the Divine lead is practiced.

In a world that feels more insanely unstable by the day, folks wanted a step-by-step way to feel enoughness. Most of all, they wanted to be able to stop agonizing about abundance. The irony was not lost on me that through God's exquisite sense of comedy, people were coming to the former consummate Catastrophe Queen herself for help.

Hundreds of people signed up for the initial online voyage, and we set sail together. The enthusiasm every week was electric. The longer it went on, the more excited we all got. (By the way, all the letters and most of the stories in this book are from people in the course, though some are altered for the sake of anonymity.) I saw how anyone, regardless of background, who sincerely applied the principles of Divine Source could gain a new relationship to money that *did not require manifesting a damn thing*.

By the time the voyage was over, I felt an incredibly strong pull to write this book. Its message is the opposite of *"You'll learn how to change or improve yourself."* You'll be *letting* Love *Itself* bring changes that you might have zero idea how to execute. This isn't about "I can do it!" Instead, "I, the ego, may not have a clue, but God sure does!"

You'll learn to offer all your financial problems to Love—and not just as a dry intellectual exercise. The fixation on manifesting has sadly led many people to think of God in only a utilitarian way. But luckily, She is more than a Cosmic Costco.

This isn't about co-creating, vision boarding, or writing yourself a pretend check for a million dollars from the Bank of Divinity. Instead, you'll begin to offer your money, your problems, your desires—all of it—back to Love, and you'll disentangle from the matrix of grasping and forcing. Over time, the awareness will come that this indeed is not *yours*. You'll feel part of something larger that you can serve and that longs to serve *you*.

In short, you'll become a conduit for Divine Flow. Since no individual person, place, or thing will be mistaken as your salvation, you'll become open to *how* God wants to deliver, often in ways you'd never imagine. Equally, you may open to how Spirit wants to use *you* in order to give. These are all highly learnable skills.

Now perhaps you're reading this and thinking, *Um . . . I have $38 in my bank account right now and I had to borrow the money to buy this freakin' book, so how the heck will this all happen?* (On the other hand, you may be someone who has plenty of money, yet always fears loss.)

Yet *wherever* you are financially matters not, because if you commit wholeheartedly to this process, you will move into the Divine Flow, with the idea that God *alone* is the owner and origin of all.

And then, I promise you, *everything will change*.

So WHAT'S WITH THE TITLE?

Maybe this book's title is what lured you in the first place, but it truly wasn't meant as some catchy catnip phrase. When I say, "It's not your money," holy mama, I mean it.

It really isn't.

And it's sure not mine, either.

It's all God's.

Perhaps the more cynical of you are thinking (as a radio host once said to me), "That's not even possible! Are you on crack? If someone stole your car tomorrow, they'd be taking *your* vehicle. You'd be the one who'd have to deal with it!" Which is true. Yes, of course, *on one level* it's your car, your money—all of it. *But on a deeper level it is not.* That's the paradox.

Before too long, you may well sense and trust this for yourself.

Because if something—whether fate, desperation, or your best friend—drew you here, perhaps you're ready to wake up from a certain culturally induced sleepwalk. Your inner alarm clock may have gone off, saying, "Time to know that Love is the provider of all."

You may be ready, finally ready, to *be* abundance rather than *chase* it.

I'll take you through specific steps to help this shift happen. The original course was eight weeks, and I strongly suggest you follow suit and carve out the same amount of time. Because the limiting beliefs most people carry can be so entrenched, eight weeks will feel long enough for the brain to shift yet short enough to keep you inspired.

Don't forget: Little by little, as you serve Love, you'll start to feel that you're being taken care of. Trust will develop that every true need will be met.

For me—and many who have followed these principles—discovering that this fear could abate was like getting early parole on a life sentence. Since it's not *your* money, but God's, you don't have to stress, strategize, plot, or manifest to make it all happen.

Anything gained through the ego can be lost, but when you're part of the Flow, God can use *anything* and *anyone* to provide. The right actions and connections can come from anywhere. Something larger than the ego can finally take over, and if your soul needs something, *it will come.*

The power of constant incoming grace, the joy of receiving, the arrival of synchronicity after synchronicity like crashing waves onto the sacred shore of your life—now that is *true abundance.*

A WORD ON TERMINOLOGY

Before we dive in, I need to address two issues.

#1 SO WHAT ABOUT GOD?

I've found that many people need permission to rewrite old language so that it feels empowering. For some, the word *God* is laden with such emotional and historical baggage that it triggers only shame, fear, and guilt. A woman wrote me that she was troubled by the idea of a Divine plan, since growing up as a strict Catholic in the '60s, to her, *plan* meant *suffering*. She was wondering if by *Divine*, I actually meant *Infinite Goodness* instead of Cosmic Punisher.

Yes, indeed. I suggested she use the term of her choice. Or *Love*. Or *Eternity*. Or maybe *the Flow*. Or even one of my favorites, the Sanskrit *Shakti*, the Supreme Force that animates all creation. To me, it doesn't matter. The name is a holder for what, in the end, is incomparable and unnamable.

Everyone is different. If you have an affinity with a particular deity, you could use Its name. For example, some offer to Jesus, Buddha, or Lakshmi, the shimmering Devi of Abundance from India, while others see

God as formless light. Some prefer *Goddess* to escape the 2,000-year-old noose of patriarchal language, while still others relate to the idea of the Beloved, in the way of Sufi poets like Rumi.

Some folks like myself find words like *God, Lord, Divine*, or *Spirit* to be protective and comforting. However, I see them without gender, so I interchange *He* and *She* often. I'll mostly use these, but I'll sprinkle in others as well. Please do what you need to make this language supportive, personal, and inviting.

Choosing words that resonate may also help if you're spiritually curious but averse to conventional religion. Don't worry, you can still learn to trust the Flow. I have a friend who truly lives the ideas of offering, surrender, and openness—but considers herself a solid agnostic. Yet she moves with faith, deferring to something beyond the ego. Often, she calls this the Way, from the Tao Te Ching.

A master surfer once told me at Ocean Beach, "You listen inside, bow to the Force, and ride that mama as far as it will go. No ego can impose itself on the sea. . . . Those who try eventually must crash and burn. It's unavoidable."

This route of offering is just like that. It's neither about passivity nor weakness, but instead honors this primal power.

For me, the Divine is *internal* as well as *external*. It is Love, and it is *All*, and certainly not some cranky, judgmental Thor in the sky hurling lightning bolts and throwing tantrums. This path is about invoking your own inner Great Self to take the wheel. What a nightmare if God were only an outer authority figure. The powerful changes that inevitably arise come from inviting an ever-deepening intimacy with this Love.

In her beautiful book *Dying to Be Me*, Anita Moorjani described the awareness that came from her near-death experience. She said, "I became conscious that there isn't an external creation separate from me—because the word *external* suggests separation and duality. . . . Although I've been using the words *Universal energy*, I can just as easily say *chi*, *prana*, or *ki*. These words mean 'life-force energy.' . . . In a nutshell, it's the Source of life, and it runs through every living thing. In fact, it fills the entire universe and is inseparable from it."

I wholeheartedly concur.

#2: AND WHAT ABOUT ALL THESE PRAYERS?

My last book, *Change Me Prayers*, was filled with petitions for transformation. And like the word *God*, everyone had an opinion about this! Some adored the idea of Love changing us to release false identifications and inhibitions, and some hated it. Occasionally, a reader would scold me: "I don't *want* to be changed. It took me forever to realize I'm good just as I am." So let me explain this idea too.

The purpose of the prayers in this book is to help you move outside the limitations of ego. Rather than twisting you into something you're *not*, they actually let you become *more* of your true Self. Inviting the Divine to take over can often unleash a freedom and spontaneity that *no amount of striving can*. Your own instinctive inner Self shows the right actions at the right time and acts through you. It's just waiting to be invited.

I began to use Change Me prayers when my beloved mother, Debbie, was in her final weeks on Earth. Beside myself with grief and wishing to bolt every second, I began to pray to be able to stay in the room with her skeletal body and give what she needed. *Change me, God, into one who can stay present and be here for her!* To my amazement, this worked like magic. Soon I discovered these prayers were powerful for *almost anything.*

That being said, please play with the language to suit your temperament. If the words *change me* are annoying, replace them with *help me, allow me,* or *let me.* Or whatever else. I mean, I personally get very excited by the idea of Divine Love transforming the heck out of me to let His plan—not the ego's—take over. But if *you* don't, other words will work. What matters is making the invitation in a way that's personal, authentic, and intimate. The exact language is secondary.

WEEK ONE

A Total Relief

*When you are no longer attached to anything
you have done your share.*

— Nisargadatta Maharaj, *I Am That*

In your first week, please read this chapter and consider where in your own life you might apply its main ideas. Understanding these concepts will prepare you for Week Two, where you'll begin the five active steps toward being Abundance.

⑦HE FULL ABUNDANCE CHANGE ME PRAYER

The first concept will be your full-on secret weapon. It reliably calls in the transformative power of Love and elevates one's consciousness—no matter *what* your current state. It invokes Abundance itself—including gratitude, prosperity, and freedom—yet it serves an even deeper purpose. It *teaches your whole Being that you, too, deserve to receive.* In many ways, it's a song of worthiness.

Divine Beloved, allow me to give with complete ease and abundance, knowing that You are the unlimited Source of all.

Let me be an easy, open conduit for Your prosperity.

Let me trust that all my own needs are always met in amazing ways

and that it's safe to give freely as my heart guides.

And equally, let me feel wildly open to receiving.

May I know my own value, beauty, and worthiness without question.

Let me allow others the supreme pleasure of giving to me.

May I feel worthy to receive in every possible way.

Change me into one who can fully love, forgive, and accept myself

So I may carry Your Light without restriction.

Let everything that needs to go, go.

> *Let everything that needs to come, come.*
> *I am utterly Your own.*
> *You are me, I am You, we are One.*
> *All is well.*

As a practice, please read this prayer every day for the full eight weeks of this process. It's a strengthening tea that needs time to steep within you.

It seems to know how to heal and strengthen various parts of your spiritual system, no matter who you are. For example, while some people—especially women—are comfortable giving, they haven't a clue how to receive. Some will give—even insanely *over*-give—then feel red-hot fury about not getting *back*. This prayer instills the intention that You. Too. Can. Receive.

For other people, the prayer softens past resentments or releases impacted bitterness. It can help ease shame around financial mistakes from the past. For still others who fear giving, it can unclench the hands from grasping and dissolve outgrown beliefs and ancient resentments.

I said the Full Abundance Change Me Prayer every day, writing it out on a piece of paper that I taped on my bathroom mirror. Throughout the day, every time I looked at myself, I said it out loud. Sometimes I even whispered it. Eventually I knew it by heart in my soul. But I can say that even after the first day, I felt a dramatic change. I was finally able to breathe, as if the prayer created space in my chest. Many other financial changes followed.

Several basic ideas run like a river through this book. They are Divine Source, Doership, Offering, and

Prarabdha Karma. Becoming familiar with them right from the start will make the whole process so much easier.

RELAXING INTO DIVINE SOURCE

Divine Source is the idea that no person, place, or thing is your salvation, only Love Itself. You begin to trust the universal storehouse that is the foundation of all. You sense the One that underlies the illusion of multiplicity in this world. You know the right next door will open at the right time and actions will spontaneously arise *as you need them.*

Let me share a couple stories illustrating this.

RELEASING THE EX

My friend Jane was filled with constant resentment about a divorce settlement she'd received many years back. She kept replaying the events in her mind, often lying awake at night, furious that she hadn't snared a better deal. But her rage perpetuated a state of stagnant victimization and created a ring of fire that actually blocked the good.

When she began to use the Abundance prayer to reinstall God as her Source, slowly, over time, she came to feel acceptance. (She also had a ton of anger to release, but more about that in Week Five.) *She came to see that her ex was not her Source.* God had simply *used him* as a partial support, but could now use anything. She stopped blocking *all the other ways* God might wish to give to her. Within a few months, Jane—who's a mechanical engineer—was handed a plum job opportunity out of the blue, far beyond anything she'd ever imagined.

My Baba

Here's another way to see Divine Source. When I was little, my grandmother Baba would come by twice a month to take me out to lunch. She was from the "old country," Polish-Russian, and parts of life here never made sense to her.

Every time we got to the huge parking lot near the restaurant, Baba would say with utter conviction, "Okay, ve need to vemember zat ve parked next to zat nice green car, darlink. So ve don't get lost!!!"

And yet, after lunch, *every* time, we'd wander the rows of cars totally dazed and confused—because her orientation point had moved. After a few weeks, I finally realized we needed a new system ("Um, Baba, we're on the second row from the entrance!").

So, that's what discovering Divine Source is like. Most people find their sense of security from whatever transient anchor is nearby. They pretend, *Okay, this particular job is my total Source. If I don't have it, I'll never find another.* Or, *This partner is my lifeline. If she ever leaves me, I'll be destroyed.*

But when you make Divine Intelligence your foundation, you finally have a fixed star to follow. You're no longer saying "this" or "that" is your answer. God knows what's needed.

You're grounded in the idea, *The perfect solution is already selected. I'll be guided to it in the right time and way. If something needs to end, the new route will come, and I will gladly follow.*

Letting Source Lead

If you think of the Divine as your ultimate protection, the Source of your work, finances, and all needs, then even the economy becomes irrelevant (as insane as I know that sounds, but stick with me for a bit). You lift your vibration *above* the turbulence of the current economic reality into the capable hands of That from Which All Things Come.

Then the Universe can use *anything* it wishes to meet your needs, sometimes in ways far more creative and unexpected than the mind can fathom. When my friend Andy says he envies people with inheritances, I often laugh. "Well, Divine Source actually *is* the ultimate trust fund. In more ways than one!"

Here's a good prayer to help rest in this awareness:

Change me, Divine Beloved, into one who fully trusts that all true needs are always met through your bounty. Let me surrender and allow You to be my Source for All. Let me breathe, relax, and let you lead. I am safe. I am peaceful. All needs will abundantly be met. I am Yours completely.

Doership

Eventually, in some life or another, chasing and grasping begin to constrict like outgrown clothes. The soul longs for something larger than the ego's agenda to guide the way. You long to serve and harmonize with the Tao.

Many times, this shift comes purely from exhaustion. A friend of mine once told me, "You know, I was a hard nut to crack, but I'm finally letting go. Who knows whether it's evolution or exhaustion, but I am!" When that time dawns, no matter *what* suffering is the spur, it's a blessed moment. You are finally being broken open . . . by God.

Releasing doership means that rather than striving and pushing harder, you actually learn to get out of the way. Your instincts start to guide your actions, and you don't cling to outcomes.

I encountered a big round of doership when I was beginning this book. My earlier works had all been collections of stories or poetry, but when I began to get the incessant message to write about abundance, I knew it had to be a real how-to book. A collection of stories, however engaging, would *not* cut it. I'd have to let God carry me far, far outside "my" own comfort zone and into the new.

Though I'd offered it all, there was still some part that remained a doer. I'd fallen into the trance of "It's my book," with all its attendant limitations. I kept saying, "I can't do this. I'm just a storyteller at heart." I became so stuck, that for a few months I couldn't write at all, even with the deadline fast approaching.

In desperation, I fully cast the burden back to God. "Free me from the illusion of doership!" I begged with every cell of my Being. The next morning, as I was awakening, I heard inside, "The Lord is my mind, I shall not falter. She does all the writing. Release the *I* and just take dictation."

It was as if Love said, "Stop bothering me about what *kind* of writer you are; that's all an illusion. Become receptive and let Me use you." As I did, the constricted husk of small self-identification cracked open, allowing the book to fly.

The importance of releasing doership continued to show itself throughout the writing of this book. I've often gotten solutions by walking. I learned early on as a writer that if I went for a long, rambling hike where I asked Love to bring what was needed, not only would ideas pour in, but signs and messages as well. A billboard here, meaningful graffiti there, maybe a random snippet of overheard conversation. I'd often stop to make notes in my phone.

One day I was strolling on Valencia Street in San Francisco when a tsunami of ideas poured in. My phone had run out of juice, so I dashed into a café for a napkin, then scribbled against a wall like a madwoman. I couldn't wait to get home to type it all up.

But when I walked a couple miles back to the car, I saw that the napkin was gone. God only knows where I'd dropped it. The panic I recalled so well from "screwing up" as a kid swelled inside. Then I remembered: *The entire walk has been offered. In fact, the whole book too. If the napkin has vanished, no worries. The Force that brought the ideas the first time can bring them again, if needed.*

I sat in the car, breathing and praying. Then, lo and behold, all the inspirations returned like a flock of seagulls. I have no doubt that they would have been blocked by fear, despair, or a rousing chorus of "How careless could you be?" Instead, the release of doership handled it all.

The great Martha Graham once said to the dancer and choreographer Agnes de Mille, "There is a vitality, a life force . . . that is translated through you into action, and because there is only one of you in all of time, this expression is unique. And if you block it, it will never exist through any other medium and it will be lost. The world will not have it. It is not your business to determine how good it is nor how valuable nor how it compares with other expressions. *It is your business to keep it yours clearly and directly, to keep the channel open!*" (italics added)

Many of you have likely felt how inspiration can come from a relaxed state of openness. That *is* the release of the doer. Even Michelangelo supposedly said his masterpiece

David was created by simply chipping away the stone that wasn't needed.

Michelangelo followed the Divine lead.

Luckily, this lead shows itself in many arenas, including money.

GOOD-BYE TO *MY*

Offering is the heart of this book.

It's handing any burden—whether a desire, attachment, illness, finances, or anything—*back* to God. After all, it was Hers to begin with! In a way, doing so says, "This is persecuting me so much, I can no longer lean on my ego's own strength. Please show me Your will."

True offering takes what can be an unbearable cross and returns it to Love. It untangles you from the seemingly inescapable thicket of doership. One easy way to begin is simply by replacing *my* with *the*. We're taught to think of *my money, my body, my partner, my happiness, my failure*. Even *my* awakening. In Western culture, the trance of *my* is king. But here's the catch: If it all belongs to *you* (the ego), the burden is all yours as well.

With the simple substitution of *the*, grasping softens, and offering begins.

Take, for example, "I'm worried right now about *this* business . . . and I'm thrilled to be offering all to Love for the right actions to be shown at the right time."

This can be applied to anything. Sally had built an entire agonizing identity centered around her terrible rheumatoid arthritis, which is so easy to do. She was always saying, "my illness," "my restrictions," "my expenses about all this" with increasing anger and desperation. I suggested that since she had nothing to lose, she could offer the entire mess to the Divine and release the *my*.

She began to say, "I give this illness fully to You. Please, please make me open and show me the right actions. And if there's *not* currently a solution, please at least let me *accept this* for now and make clear what I need to learn."

She immediately felt more spacious simply from dropping that *my*. And over time, the process of offering, acceptance, and disentanglement brought healing she'd never imagined. She felt guided to return to an acupuncturist she'd seen many years before who used treatments, herbs, and diet. However, this time it all worked, perhaps because she'd finally released the grip of *her ego's identification with the problem*. Although flare-ups still come, she's much improved.

RADICAL ACCEPTANCE

A part of Sally's process was acceptance. While this idea is currently popular, it can be far easier to invite through prayer than by trying to convince the ego to accept what it hates. This means praying to embrace *something As It Is in the now*. Not forever, just *right now*, since in God's world, things can turn on a dime.

Radical acceptance in the Now opens the Flow.

The concept that "whatever you resist, persists" has some truth. One of the greatest revelations of my life was that I could pray for this radical allowing, especially when stuck in total resistance. I could say, "Let me embrace this only for the *moment*. Let me say yes just for now." Acceptance is neither resignation nor powerlessness, but an opening of the Way for the next right actions.

OFFERING RESENTMENT TO THE DIVINE

Sara is a well-known painter with a rabid following. For many years, she made a good living showing her work in galleries around the world. Then she met Joelle, the great love of her life.

In a classic whirlwind romance, within three months of meeting, Joelle had moved into Sara's San Francisco home. However, she had no steady source of income; her last partner had carried her financially as well. As "in love" as Sara was, she soon simmered with anger about taking care of her. In fact, as the months went by, Sara became more and more enraged about playing the financial caretaker.

Yet instead of setting some healthy boundaries, Sara clung more tightly to the relationship. As furious as she was, she still didn't want to lose it. Then the oddest thing began to occur.

During their first year together, the sale of Sara's artwork ground to a standstill. The retreats she taught around the world stopped filling as well. She couldn't fathom what was happening until one day, she understood.

Her resentment toward Joelle, combined with grasping to keep her at all costs, had dammed the flow of abundance. Sara was blocking it to avoid supporting her partner!

When she finally offered her painting, finances, and relationship back to the Divine, Sara became clear. She knew she needed a self-sufficient partner and could no longer carry Joelle. She offered the relationship back to the Divine and let go.

A couple months after they broke up, her finances went back to normal.

The act of offering is a holy process. Anything truly surrendered is indeed made sacred. You're not just throwing some mess at God, saying, "Hey, I hope *You* can handle it, dude, 'cause I sure can't!" You're no longer demanding, "How fast can I get my order delivered?" Instead you're softening and wondering, *What am I learning here? How can I be kinder to myself right now?* You take that unbearable burden and say, "I can no longer be an ego lugging this around like a pack mule. Please show me the way!"

And often you find that the problem that's been your biggest nemesis is actually the key to your freedom.

You end up in the *present*, trusting there will be enough. You're not obsessed about what you must manifest next, or how great life will be later. You're not fixated on past regrets or a fantasy future. You're smack in the present, accepting the Now and open to Love.

This can be done anytime, anywhere, right in the middle of this frenzied world, in a traffic jam or at the gym. There's no need for a cave in Nepal. No matter where you are, offering brings you back where you belong, right into God's lap. You say, "May this burden that's brought me such suffering become the road to You."

And it will be.

I once read an interview with a guy from Ecuador who was called the world's greatest hitchhiker. He'd written copiously about the 2,000 rides he'd caught, traveling over 100,000 miles through 90 countries.

But here's what I found fascinating: Radical acceptance was his secret. On days when he felt frustrated and impatient by the side of the road, he was always stuck the longest. And on days when he felt open and accepting, even despite bad weather or any other problem, the rides pulled up quickly, sometimes within moments.

He'd also discovered that this acceptance worked not only with hitching, but with romance as well. For a long time, he'd doubted he'd ever find a partner adventurous enough for life on the road. When he gave up looking and accepted his solitude, she finally found him. They've been circling the globe together ever since.

OFFERING AND MONEY

From day one, we're taught that all finances belong to ego. The message is constant: "It's *my* money. How can I get more? Why do I spend like this? Why am I terrified of loss every minute?"

But when all is offered to the Divine, the focus becomes "Okay, God, I hand this fear of loss to You. Free me from these worries. Show me the first step. I'm ready to know Divine Source!"

New resources start to arrive because you're finally open. You're no longer saying, "This is *my* disaster and I'll punish myself forever for creating it." Or "I'll be furious for all eternity at anyone who put me here." You're ready to release the past, arrive in the Now, and make the Divine your Source.

The more you release blame, resentment, and shame, the more your inner door will open. You begin to feel a sense of oneness with everything rather than just chasing the next mirage of safety.

Offering can be applied to anything, big or small. My friend Gayle was once fretting about whether to go to a certain yoga retreat in Costa Rica. It was crazy expensive, and she was already hugely in debt. Every day she vacillated about it; she wanted to go, but didn't want to be reckless.

But what a perfect opportunity for offering. Rather than getting into an ego wrestling match about yes or no, she could offer the retreat completely to God. She could say, "Okay, I'd love this, but show me Your will! If I'm meant to attend, make it clear. But if not, let me be fine *with or without* it."

After she offered, Gayle felt a huge wave of relief about not going. Instead she heard about an interesting one-day workshop coming straight to her town. She knew this was her sign to stay put till some of the debt was cleared. (I also loved that she wasn't pretending Divine Source means you just burn through money on any old thing, assuming God will replace the bounty. Every case is different, as we'll explore later.)

You may be reading this and thinking, *Oh honey, you have no idea. I've got way, way bigger problems than some silly yoga retreat.* But here's the truth; offering is a muscle. If you practice it with the small stuff, it will aid you with the big.

PRARABDHA KARMA

One of my favorite spiritual writers had a time when multiple illnesses plagued him. Someone said to me, "This guy is a total beam of light. You feel uplifted simply by being in the same room. So how can even *he* have all these problems?"

One of the dark legacies of manifestation culture is that many people think we attract *every* single blessed thing. They assume if only we perfect ourselves enough, we gain VIP entry to a secret Disneyland where nothing "bad" ever occurs.

And then they blame themselves when the inevitable challenges come that are a part of incarnate existence. Or they harshly judge others when difficulties arrive, assuming they *must* have done wrong. Some of them even coldly say, "Oh, pity she created that. But me, *I'm* different!"

But here's what's missing. While the Law of Attraction is true, so is the Law of Prarabdha Karma. I mean, even the great Indian saint Ramakrishna got throat cancer. Or look at Jesus. He didn't exactly die drinking margaritas in the Bahamas. What matters is how we handle our unique Prarabdha Karma, our own soul's course of study. When embraced, it becomes the royal road to true abundance.

MILLION-DOLLAR MYSTERY TOUR

Did you ever hear about how the actor Jim Carrey wrote himself a check for $10 million from the Universal Bank long before he was famous? It spawned a parade of similar check writers all over the planet. Unfortunately, however, many came to believe their own gazillions didn't arrive FedEx Express because they'd blocked it. Yet I'd say it happened for Jim simply because that was *his* Prarabdha Karma.

This book comes from a singular premise: *Everybody has a different set of abundance lessons they're learning in any given lifetime.* It may not be your own destiny to have $10 million. That might actually be the last thing your soul needs! You might be learning this life to trust you'll always have enough . . . and the more you open to Divine Source, the more you will.

Some issues are so fundamental to our soul's awakening that we come back lifetime after lifetime to resolve them. Someone who accrues great wealth may be working out a certain karma—perhaps to see if they'll be generous, grateful, and good-hearted with their largesse. If they're not, they may well create a *different* karma in future lives.

The Law of Attraction and the Law of Prarabdha Karma intertwine in every moment.

The more you come to trust this Source, the less you'll *need* vast wealth to feel abundant. If it comes, then fantastic, and perhaps you'll be generous with it. But, you start feel prosperous no matter *what* your personal Prarabdha Karma.

This also makes it easier to feel acceptance and compassion. A teacher of mine used to say, "Be grateful for the karma you don't have. Your own is plenty!"

I'm constantly struck by how resting in Divine Source is independent of wealth. Some insanely prosperous clients I've had were in constant mental torture, while some who lived month-to-month had such faith they rarely worried at all. They lived in a state of grace, where everything needed arrived like clockwork.

Now one last point. For some of you, the eight weeks of this journey may make your money increase quickly. You may suddenly have much—and I mean, *much, much—* more. But for others, while the dollars may not immediately grow, something else will in the most beautiful way.

Your trust.

You start to feel at the deepest level of your being that one way or another, perhaps for the first time in your life—*every true need will be met.*

The right solutions for any financial problems will become obvious . . . and if you need something, it will come.

INTENTION

Intention is a part of the puzzle that's often misunderstood. In Sanskrit the beautiful word *sankalpa* means a one-pointed resolve to focus on a specific goal. You could see it as a solemn vow formed by the heart and mind. In a sense, it means "You are what you focus on."

Indeed, sankalpa is an invaluable tool. I now offer this journey fully to Love. May everything that's ready to open, open. May everything that's ready to leave, leave. I long for the Highest to occur. May I be Abundance."

These types of intentions make *space* for the Divine will. They're so very different from goals like "I *will* make a million dollars by February" or "My soul mate *will* come in 30 days." Once you start to trust this Source, you stop *insisting* every passing desire must happen; you relax and know that one way or the other, your needs will be covered.

This can feel like getting a 400-pound manifesting monkey off your back.

To be clear, I'm not dismissing the power of the mind. For example, plenty of athletes have successfully used visualization and positive thoughts to enhance performance. And surely if you're someone who habitually complains all day, positive thought is a huge improvement over negative. We'll even use some in the abundance process. Nonetheless, intention without surrender can be a fast path to delusion.

Take this story from one of my favorite shows, *This American Life*. Once, the cast of *Riverdance*, a well-known musical, bought a batch of tickets when the mega-millions lottery climbed into the stratosphere. A cast member who knew visualization assured everyone that if they believed strongly enough, winning would be inevitable. After all, that was the power of intention: Dream it and it will come! They just needed to *feel* that they'd already won.

But as the week went on, they all got more and more obsessed with elaborate plans for how to spend their money. They even did a frenzied chant of "Lotto, lotto, lotto" during the final performance before the drawing. (Oh, to have been a totally befuddled audience member for that one!)

But then when they gathered for the drawing, chilled champagne at the ready, not a single number matched. Of course, they were devastated. Their intention had been pure and ferocious.

Yet, isn't it simple? It wasn't their time to win. It wasn't their Prarabdha Karma.

I often laugh when someone says you have to know what you intend to create or God will be confused. As if the Supreme-Power-that-Created-All doesn't know precisely what's needed.

When someone asks what my intentions are I often say, "Oh, you know, just one: that God takes over entirely and brings Her will."

Prayer for Transforming Money

Okay, God, open me.

I'm ready.

I don't want the exhausting burden of this topic anymore!

I am done.

Open me to whatever I'm meant to receive from this sacred process.

Help me let go of any old beliefs and feelings that get in the way of Your plan for my life. May I know the good I can do as an embodiment of Divine abundance.

Many of the money-focused books and courses out there are based on the idea "How can I get more? I want it *all*, and I *deserve* it!"

But this is a wholly other way.

So right here, right now, before we launch into the daily five steps, you can bless the entire process of opening to abundance with a direct prayer.

> Change me. Open me.
>
> Make me receptive to the unexpected.
>
> May I receive all that is meant for me over these next weeks and beyond.
>
> Let me know my own worthiness to receive.
>
> Let me play with these new ideas as an adventure.
>
> And then, let me embrace what happens according to Your will.
>
> I am Yours. You are mine. We are One. All is well.

Okay, let's start those steps!

THE 5 DIVINE STEPS

*Be the One that changes everyone's luck
when you walk in the room.*

— attributed to Hafiz

Please begin this week doing these five steps. I ask you to do them every day for the remaining weeks. They don't have to take long, and soon you will find a momentum with them.

STEP I:
SAY THE FULL ABUNDANCE CHANGE ME PRAYER

This invocation can reliably lift you out of scarcity and worry into receptivity. Even if you're in a bad mood when you say it, you may be surprised by what happens.

Over the years, thousands of people have written to me describing the relief it can bring, sometimes instantly. But if it feels at first as if you're doing it mechanically, don't worry. It may take a little time to fully resonate.

After a week or two, you may feel yourself stepping into this prayer, your voice resonating with the words. You may sense them vibrating inside you, melting resistance and fear. Let me reassure you, no matter who you are, this *can* occur. Try to be as fully present as you can while you say it. Stick with it even if cash isn't flying through the air ducts the minute you finish.

Invite Love to do the work and open you to both give and receive easily. (Since this isn't self-help, no need to slave away to change yourself; God will do what you cannot.)

I mentioned earlier that praying to be changed allowed me to be there for my mom in a miraculous and unexpected way I never could have imagined. Love came to the rescue, and obliged. Never underestimate what might occur for you too.

I've kept this on my computer since the course began. When I open it each day, I feel like I have a waiting friend. This morning, as I sat here annoyed about paying bills, I read the prayer again. Suddenly my consciousness imploded! I saw that I was actually distributing God's money in order to get my needs met. It was such an uplifting insight that I ran upstairs to tell my partner. Something inside is blossoming and I feel such ease. For the first time, I feel not only that there can be enough, I can imagine plenty for everything!

As you move out of scarcity and resentment into being abundance, you may find similar shifts suddenly happen. The Flow is moving through you . . . and you can always receive more.

Step 2:
Start to Clean Your House

An important part of opening to receive is *making room*. I mean that in the most practical, physical way. This. Is. Critical. Especially if you have a lot of clutter, you'll be "creating a vacuum" to allow the new to come. This clearing is actually connected to the Yoga Sutra term *saucha*, which means "purity" or "cleanliness." While it applies both to the soul and the physical space, for now we'll apply it to the latter.

I've found the easiest way to start the clearing process—especially if you have enormous resistance—is by offering. Just like money, just like anything. No need for the ego to freak out: "Oh my God, how will I make time for all this cleaning? What will I toss? What will I keep? How will I ever decide?"

Instead, right from the start, offer all your belongings to Love.
After all, every belonging comes from and returns to the Divine. What can any of us take with us on the day we die?

So perhaps you can say, "Dear Love, show me what I no longer need. Show me what needs to go." If you pray with sincerity, you *will* be shown.

The mind might protest, *How will I know?* Well, I've found with practice, the body and instincts guide you. The wonderful Marie Kondo was right when she said in *The Life-Changing Magic of Tidying Up,* release what doesn't bring you joy. But even that advice leaves some people unsure, so knowing how to offer seriously helps. You may feel yourself drawn to start at a certain spot. Maybe it will be one particular drawer in your kitchen, maybe it'll be your clothes. *Trust yourself.* You could pray, "Help me listen inside during this process."

While my own physical space has always been pretty tidy, my computer used to be an ongoing nightmare. One day, I finally offered the whole thing, praying, "I have such resistance to organizing this. Show me where the hell to begin before I lose my mind!" (Yes, that was my plea. No need to hide your feelings from Love, who knows you completely anyway. Sometimes I imagine the Divine smiling at my hotheaded prayers of frustration.) Moments later, I started deleting four years of email.

Love will show your own holy starting line.

You may well head to that one closet that actually ends up being the key to your prosperity. Maybe 10 years ago you shoved old love letters there from someone you're still mad at. Perhaps finally burning, blessing, and releasing those will be your own personal portal to abundance.

I've seen this happen. Your home may have symbolic pockets of pus that simply have to be drained. When you ask Love to show you, It will. If you've got massive resistance (some people fear releasing anything at all), you can say, "Let a freakin' miracle happen so that I may make space for the New!"

Some of you may also need to start smaller than your home. You could start with your car, wallet, or purse. If you're on the road, you could even reorganize your suitcase. Anything can be a symbolic and powerful beginning. As the musician John Cage once famously said, "Begin anywhere."

In truth, many people find the process infectious and unstoppable once they dive in. You may even discover ways to make it more pleasurable with music or little gifts you give yourself as you go.

But here's what's most important. When you offer the process and stop trying to clean from your ego's limited strength, Something Else steps in. The Divine begins to act *through* you and *for* you. Holiness itself makes the space.

STEP 3: STOP COMPLAINING ABOUT MONEY

Whether your tendency is to complain to yourself or to others, just *stop* for these weeks.

Notice when you begin to say things like "I wish I could buy that, but I don't have the money. I'm so mad, I *never* have it." As an experiment, just *stop* all that for now.

When I shared this idea with a friend, she bristled. "Well, I won't censor myself. I like to be authentic."

"But you're not censoring." I giggled. "You're leaving room for a new, more abundant existence. That's harder if you're constantly feeding yourself poison."

You may have no idea how much constant statements like "I'm always broke" or "I'm always strapped" can impact life. Even the words themselves are dark and heavy. *Broke. Strapped.* This is the part of the Law of Attraction that's true. In Sanskrit, it's called the *Matrika Shakti*, the magical attracting power of language.

So for the duration of this course, take a break from scarcity language, even if you still believe it. This can feel like the cessation of a mental sledgehammer. You may not realize how deafening it was until you take a break.

Now, I'm not saying deny reality. At the moment, there may well be things that you can't afford. Nonetheless, for now, just stop insisting that you can't. Whenever you feel tempted, perhaps say, "Whatever I need always comes."

For example, you hear about a course you're drawn to take. While you might have once said, "Oh, I shouldn't have that. I can't afford that," for now, give it to the Divine for the highest outcome. You can say, "All my finances are offered to Love, and miraculously, whatever I need always comes. The Divine is my Source for all."

Okay, one more thing. Please don't check your bank balance every two seconds during this process, wondering, *Is it going up? Is this working?* For now, just offer, offer, offer. You're in the midst of making a serious invocation to Source. Just focus on that. The rest is God's.

You can tell the Flow *will constantly bring what's needed*, even if you don't have a clue yet how this will occur. When you need to know, you will know.

Once a guy named James wrote on my Facebook page that he was thrilled I posted so much stuff for free since he was not only broke, but proudly cheap too.

I couldn't help responding, "I'm glad you like being here, dear James. But if you keep insisting that you're both those things, you'll continue to attract scarcity and constriction as night follows day. So while you're proud you've never spent a penny here, honestly, it's nothin' to brag about."

Here's why. There's this funny thing my mom always used to say when I was little—"Don't be a *shnorer.*" In Yiddish, it's someone who wants only to take and never give. Shnorers live outside the circle of abundance, hoping that if they grab enough, they might feel safe. It never works.

But it's not hard to learn to become a conduit. Then the Universe can bring what you yourself need and *also* let you give. Then you *long* to support others who have been helpful to you. *You enter the Flow by giving back.*

Besides, while we're at it, *broke* and *cheap* are actually two different problems. *Broke* can be fixed by saying that you're "temporarily financially challenged." There's no shame in that. It's happened to the best of us!

However, *cheap* is a different story. Cheap is like saying, "I simply *won't* be a conduit for abundance. I won't spend, and I won't give."

You have to want to let God *use* you to give. You have to want to be part of the Flow, not only financially, but in every way.

To quote *Outrageous Openness*:

So give some things away.

Pay for some friends' meals.

Do whatever it takes to feel prosperous

despite current appearances.

And never, ever say you're broke.

If you dwell in the vibration of fear, doubt,

and constriction

that you will undoubtedly continue to attract.

If you continue to insist you never

have enough,

the world will heartily agree.

But if you let yourself be

what you think you need,

one way or another,

it will come.

STEP 4:
MAKE A STATEMENT OF GRATITUDE

Each day, simply find *one* thing you're grateful for rather than fixating on what you wish was happening instead. I'm sure many of you may have worked with this idea before, but it's especially powerful with the other steps.

You don't have to make a big list; you don't have to journal about gratitude for 20 hours. You don't have to pretend to be glad for something that you're not. You can keep it real. Just *one thing* each day, even if it's your hot coffee or your old, comfortable slippers. Maybe it'll be different each day. Let the feeling permeate you. This practice changes neurotransmitters in your brain so that the ones that say *thank you* become more active and the ones that complain are diminished.

STEP 5:
SAY "IT'S EASY FOR ME TO RECEIVE."

Every day.

Some of you may be thinking, *Oh man, it's the hardest thing in the world for me to receive! I feel overwhelming guilt when people give to me or I spend money on myself.*

If that's true for you, maybe start by saying, "Amazingly, somehow, through the miraculous intervention of Love Itself, it's *suddenly* easy for me to receive."

As an experiment, drop the resistance. Say it however you need to say it. You can even get playful:

> *Every day, God makes me more open to receive.*
>
> *What a miracle, that I, of all people, am finally open to receive!*
>
> *How the heck did this happen? I'm suddenly open!*
>
> *I am ready. Receiving gets easier every day.*
>
> *I am one with this expansive Source of all.*
>
> *Everything I need always comes, and I gratefully receive.*
>
> *I am so, so damn excited to receive.*

We're focusing on ease, receptivity, and openness—the opposite of stress, struggle, and jealousy.

Most of us have been indoctrinated into this crazy cultural paradigm of incessant competition, where we're pitted against each other for even a tiny scrap of abundance. This is founded in total scarcity thinking. But as soon as you return to Source, it honestly doesn't matter what anyone else has. No one can commandeer your good.

Today at work, my boss asked what I was up to. I told her the truth: "I'm investigating how on earth I could take my elderly dad on a dream safari." To my amazement, she walked into her office and returned with an envelope.

She'd spontaneously given me the full amount! I exclaimed, "Oh no, I can't take this!"

But she insisted. "I want to give it to you, and you can. But you can only use it for the safari, and nothing else." We both laughed and hugged.

It was so hard to accept! Would I regret this later? Was it a bribe? Then a friend said, "This gift isn't for what you'll have to do, it's for what you've already done."

That's when I knew to just say, "Thank you." I'm still in shock.

I laughed, wondering, *Did I make space for this by cleaning out my home for a month like an absolute crazy person?* I think so!

Many people feel challenged opening to Spirit's generosity and largesse. In fact, occasionally you're offered something, and you really do have to intuit: Does this have strings?

You could pray, "If for some reason I'm *not* meant to take this, if there's a catch, please show me. Send me a sign and *stop* me."

(This is actually a great prayer anytime you need a Divine double-check.)

If you're not stopped, then perhaps God is *using* that person to give to you, and you know, She can use anyone. I'm not ignoring that there are psychic vampires who will give to hook you. But if you offer it over, you'll be shown—those will feel sticky, so you'll say no. But if it feels "clean," without an agenda, you're getting yet another chance to receive God's bounty. The cleaning—along with all the rest of these practices—can indeed help open the way.

Just engrave "It's easy for me to receive" in your heart. You. Will. Be. Changed.

A Meditation to Begin Your Journey

I've found that Love really communicates through the instincts, and especially through the body. It feels welcomed through meditation and prayer.

Have someone else read this out loud for you, or perhaps record your own voice and play it back so you can enter it fully. (In addition, if you'd like a recording of my voice reading the prayer, go to "Resources" at the back of book.)

Focusing on your breath, feel yourself sinking into the earth, your body heavy and relaxed.

However you envision it, imagine your own finances, your money, even if you feel as if you have little.

Get a clear symbolic picture of your finances in your mind's eye.

Now, imagine that you're taking this symbol to Love itself, however you envision it.

Feel that you're now offering this burden to the Divine and that you're saying, "Make me ready."

I'm ready to be shown.

I'm ready to open to this, and I'm ready to have this belong to you.

I'm ready to allow old restrictions, constraints, limits, and baggage to go.

Take me over and begin to do what my own ego never could.

Take me over and begin to allow this change!

Let me be uplifted and transformed.

Imagine yourself offering the entire burden of your finances to that Force of Love.

You may see a word; you may hear something; you may just feel it. Know that whatever torture you've felt over money can finally be offered to God. What a relief.

You're finally really offering it, and you're asking to be shown the right actions, from today onward. Those right actions will be shown, step-by-step, from the inside, all in right timing.

And then, as you're ready, slowly come back out. Jot down anything that may have happened. Even the smallest message may turn out to be important.

YOU CAN BE REAL

If you systematically go through these steps over these weeks, a certain terror—that I myself knew every single blessed day growing up—will lessen. It may not be fully dissolved by the end of this process, but it will decrease, possibly sooner than you expect.

It may even be diminished simply from reading this far. Actually, you may even have felt a shift just from reading the book's title alone.

I was working one day in an Oakland café when the guy next to me saw a mock-up of the cover on my desktop. Glancing at the title, he exclaimed, "Dude, are you kidding? I *need* that! Money is my biggest burden."

When you cast off that burden of *your*, you lay down the world's hugest weight.

Okay, one last thing. You don't have to put a happy face on all this. Later in this book, we'll deal with emotions like anger, shame, sadness, and fear that may need to be felt. Don't worry, we'll get there. We'll work with them, even by breaking, smashing, or burning things for release, if needed. It can be critical to feel . . . and let go.

But for now, especially if you have anger or shame about financial issues, just let it be. Today is the day, once and for all, that you start to hand your finances to the Divine.

At this juncture, you're preparing for just one thing: to become a vehicle for abundance. As you keep doing the steps, you'll notice synchronicities increase. You'll start to be in the right place at the right time to freely give and receive and to help others when you're guided. All may spontaneously start to happen without much thought.

You'll move into a grace-filled, expansive reality where you remember that you're an unlimited Being guided by Love and a vehicle for Divine Source.

No matter who you are.

WEEK THREE

DEEPENING

You can't water the roses if you're standing
on the garden hose.

— Jill Wolk

Now that you've completed the second week, how do you feel? Have you received boons like the return of a lost object or the sudden repayment of a debt? Or is the main shift a palpable feeling of relief? Or maybe have old feelings arisen, causing you to feel sad or nostalgic? That can happen too. Wherever you are, let it be. Just keep going. More will be revealed!

In Week Three, we'll be deepening into the five steps. And let me tell you, here's one of the most delicious parts of this process. While initially you have to stay focused and use the tools, the more you practice, *they* begin to *use you*. They gain a life of their own.

Sometimes I think becoming abundance means unblocking the hose that the Divine flows through. It's easy to get all twisted about a topic like money, but God knows exactly how to open you. To be used as a conduit for abundance, many things often have to be released. A feeling of unworthiness may be the block, or perhaps resentment, fear, or anger. Or attachments to people who only bring self-doubt and negativity. We'll be working with all of that.

If you diligently continue this process over time, the hose will start to open and the water that's waiting to come through indeed will. With abandon. That's when the fun really begins.

ENGAGE FULLY

When I was teaching the course, many people dove into this process like a river on a hot day, while others were more passive observers. While that was okay, this truly *is* meant to be a program of participation. Far less happened for those only hearing the calls while they sunned on the riverbanks. If someone wanted deep and lasting change, they had to dive in and use the tools.

So I encourage you to engage fully and let the steps carry you. Because, really, why not? Although, some of you may need to read the whole book through once and then return to start all the actions, and that's fine too.

But think about it. If you were drawn here, money has probably brought you its fair share of grief and suffering, one way or another. Perhaps some hidden part of you has been longing forever for a new solution to this ancient burden.

So what do you have to lose?

OLD SOUL ABUNDANCE

During our weeks together, be open to inviting a Divine plan—one that Love Itself may have chosen expressly for you. Stop reading everything that fills this world like New Age crabgrass about *getting more, having more,* or *being more.* For now, just drop it.

Because if you've tried and tried to get more money and found this hasn't worked, I want you to know you're in no way a "failure." Instead, *you might just be an old soul.* If you are, chasing after abundance can be fruitless and exhausting because you were born to align with Love's will, follow the Tao, and serve something beyond the ego.

As you shift from demanding and chasing to offering and opening, abundance will start to come *through* you as you're hollowed out to receive. (The connection between "hollow" and "hallow" has often struck me. Perhaps the very act of being emptied and opened makes you holy.)

Besides, if you're an old soul, nothing is gained from thinking, *Wow, I'm so powerful, I can manifest anything!*

Love Itself may respond: *Are you kidding? You're actually here to learn to open and stop blocking the Flow.*

In fact, your ego may even be *prevented* by the Divine from manifesting anything. I know mine sure was.

And though an array of coaches may line up from here to Uzbekistan to say you need more sessions, they may be dead wrong. Many old souls aren't weak, wrong, or blocking anything. The Holy One Herself may be emptying you of fear and attachments and preparing you to receive Her luminous Plan.

Letting go can be an important part of the hollowing-out process that the Divine uses. As the hands stop grasping in a clenched fist, they often can relax into an open palm to receive more than you ever imagined.

In other words, while you're busy feeling neglected, God may actually be knee-deep in Her own blessed project: your freedom. Perhaps after thousands of lifetimes.

Now don't get me wrong. This offering route is not just sunshine and lollipops. Sometimes learning to surrender is so intense you can feel as if you're dying. The ego is learning what might be the hardest thing: how to stop trying to control the whole Universe.

Yet bit by bit, it occurs. And as the Divine plan begins to sprout like a wild, lush garden after years in a desert, you may think, *I never could have imagined this, yet it feels so right. It's as if everything has prepared me for . . . right now.*

As this unfolds, you no longer force or shame yourself in the old ways. You become more and more spacious, present, and open. You start to move with the Flow Itself. In fact, "failure at manifesting" might have been the Divine plan all along—the perfect route to make you leap, once and for all, straight into Love's waiting arms.

ᗌESIRES BECOME PREFERENCES

So how does this happen? It's not that all desires simply die through this process of offering (although some do). And you sure don't blame yourself for having them in the first place, because they're part of being human. But desires themselves are never really the problem, and never have been. *Attachment* is. Through this work we'll be doing together, they'll stop holding you prisoner.

You can even say, "Dear God, I give this raging desire to You. Open me to Your will, release me from my fixations and attachments. Surprise and delight me with Your plan. You know what's needed, and I am open to receive!"

Eventually, one sublime desire takes precedence over all the others: to follow the Tao, the Divine Flow, at all costs.

STEP 1: REVISITING THE ABUNDANCE PRAYER

I don't know what Force brought this prayer through me, but I do know to the bottom of my purple-pedicured toes that it works.

If you haven't made a recording in your own voice yet, please do. *I hate my voice.* you might say, but try it anyway. What if you imagined God Herself was speaking through you?

Hearing *yourself* can dissolve the illusion that prosperity is something *external* to be chased. You can read it with intensity and focus, as if you yourself are a sacred vessel for it.

Let this enter your Being, releasing any old ideas of constriction or limitation and returning you to your true essence as expansive, radiant light. Maybe because it's the opposite of my own thoughts as a struggling, lonely kid, this prayer can still make me cry. I'm thrilled when people tell me their own children already know it.

STEP 2: CLEANING YOUR SPACE

The building of your inner vessel for receiving abundance is central. You give Love permission to change and prepare you in whatever ways are needed. Through receptivity and invitation, you're teaching your brain and body to become a conduit for the good.

By now you should be focused on cleaning your external physical space as well. This step could also be called: Hey, it's not your *stuff*, either.

Even the seemingly mundane act of cleaning becomes a sacred process once it's been offered. No matter how packed with clutter your home might currently be, you'll be building, day by day, a temple for Love. By releasing what you don't need, use, or adore, you'll make room for this Divine residency.

You don't have to stress over what to keep or release. Just try this: Open your hands toward the sky, then feel how you're offering up a massive burden.

You can say, "I don't need all the answers to every money problem yet. I'm on my way. Right now, I only need to be shown what to *release*."

The ego might say, *Oh it's all too much! I've got 14 years of clutter. How will I ever figure this all out?* But here's the other way: *Offer all your belongings to the Divine.* Think of everything you own, then say to Love: *This is all Yours, so please show me.*

Spanda: The Inner Pull

Your intuition is eager to help you do this clearing. As you continue to offer all actions, your instincts will sharpen.

You may even start to sense specific things, such as *Oh, these golf clubs blocking the closet for the last 10 years can go to Goodwill. I'm thrilled that they'll* finally *get used!*

You won't necessarily hear an inner voice speaking, but if you're open and don't second-guess yourself, you'll just *know.* Perhaps hesitantly at first, but later with more and more confidence. *You will start to trust yourself.*

Often, intuition comes through the spontaneous pull in your body that I mentioned earlier. That's the *spanda*, or inner leap. It's the pure momentum of the Shakti, the holy energy that runs through each of us. It is supremely wise, free, and indifferent to the *should*s that obsessively fill most minds. As you get pulled from spot to spot while cleaning out your space, you'll follow the tug of that spanda. Perhaps your medicine cabinet will call you at first, and then the kitchen. You'll just know.

The Fateful Turkish Rug

Many people have trouble releasing things they don't like or use because they don't want to feel they've wasted money. But part of becoming a conduit is surrendering what you no longer need so someone else can enjoy it. Even the very idea of *waste* starts to change as you open to Divine Source.

You've probably heard of the idea that nature abhors a vacuum. When you clear out what's not needed, you simply make space for what *wants* to come instead.

I wrote in *Outrageous Openness* about a woman who had a gorgeous Turkish rug in her bedroom. Although it was lush and expensive, she hated it since it came from her divorce. In fact, every time she saw it, she found herself brimming anew with hatred toward her ex. Given that it was smack next to her bed, it was hard to avoid.

As she came to understand Source, she finally decided to sell the damn thing. In her heart, she longed to be free of it, and sincerely wished someone else could enjoy it. She made a small fortune selling the rug, then excitedly used the money for a monthlong trip to Maui, where, for the first time in years, she began to feel that she truly deserved happiness.

She told me she was sure that her wholehearted release of the Rug of Resentment changed every other area of her life.

Go in Small Steps

Give yourself permission to let go of all you don't need—including those clothes you haven't worn since 1992. It's simple. Releasing them can start to clear the old stories that no longer serve you. In fact, just an hour of decluttering can help open the Flow.

Just begin. Maybe one single drawer keeps pulling you. If you go there and offer it, your path will unravel like a golden thread as you move instinctively from spot to spot. Many people are so relieved to be cleaning, they *cannot* stop once they start.

"Oh dear Lord, unbury me from all this clutter so a new life may come!"

David, a writer, dreaded pruning his massive book collection—yet knew he had to. Once he offered the process, he began to clean in small, manageable chunks. He even set a timer for an hour and wrote a prayer of release.

He plowed through nine boxes of books that had been piled so high in his bedroom they'd blocked his window for years. He chucked more than half. How symbolic that he could finally see his own view for the first time.

If you feel resistant, do what he did: Set a timer, then dive in. Maybe say, "For this hour, just take me over. Please make me ready and show me what to do!" Sometimes when I'm really unmotivated, I'll even say, "C'mon, God, use me to go kick some butt." I've found this works!

Or . . . Invite the Help

I've often prayed, "Okay, God, if you want me to do this certain seemingly impossible task, then change me into someone who can . . . or please, please bring the right help."

Some people need to hire someone to help do this clearing, and listen, there's no shame in that. Others have a trusty friend who will go through their clothes and say, "Oh my god, those plaid culottes are banished forever!"

You actually don't have to know *who* will assist, because the Divine Herself does. If you need it, it will come, or you'll be shown the right actions. Make the offering and stay open.

You could even invoke the Law of Divine Selection that Florence Scovel Shinn wrote about by saying, "The right help is already selected, and I'll be guided to it easily and gratefully."

Once you get into the habit of invoking this law, you'll trust that the right route already exists. You'll sip from the sacred chalice of aparigraha.

I've used it forever to find everything from bookkeepers to dentists, yoga teachers, jobs, apartments, and every adorable cat I've ever had. Really, it's good for anything, and particularly when you're surrounded by negative people who keep insisting you'll *never* find what's needed. But the "perfect" solution is already picked, and you'll be guided in the right time and way. Repeat whenever you waver.

When Lorna had her computer stolen with no funds to replace it, she began to pray: "Okay, God, it's Yours. If it's meant to go, help me accept this. Otherwise, the perfect solution is already selected, and I'll be guided."

The next day, someone at work said, "You know, I've got this other laptop just sitting in my closet collecting dust. Any chance you want it?"

Twenty-four hours, and problem solved.

If You Don't Live Alone
Pashma, during the course, wondered how to clean and clear a space while living with others.

She was thrilled that she had purged 30 years from file cabinets and released her unneeded clothes and shoes. She felt a certain immediate spaciousness, yet all her husband's clutter remained. What a challenge!

If a dilemma like this is offered, Love can often make a way out of no way.

If you're in the same boat, just persevere for now with your own stuff. Don't lecture or badger the other person. Focus on taking care of your own part as you continue to offer the whole mess.

Very often, the people in your home will catch the cleaning bug almost in spite of themselves. Glenda was married to someone who was a complete pack rat. She did her own clearing for a few weeks; then one day, out of nowhere, her wife, Jade, up and rented a truck. Just like that. Without a word, Jade took most of the contents of their overstuffed garage straight to Goodwill.

And that was that.

Glenda felt that Jade had been profoundly shaken on a psychic level by all her cleaning. She had created a force field that couldn't be resisted. But she never pushed Jade; it just happened.

Besides, there's always a handy prayer such as, "Okay, God, since I have the insane karma of living with this person, please take over. Let me do my share, and hand You the rest for a miracle!"

Psychic Purification

Once the home is cleaned of debris and physical clutter, you might want to burn some incense or herbs to help clear the energy. I love to open all the windows, then do an initial round of sage or camphor, or a combination of frankincense and myrhh, for cleansing. Sometimes I follow that by burning a second round of palo santo, a fragrant wood from Peru that's easy to get. For even more purification, you can also sprinkle rose water on the door thresholds and sea salt on the windowsills. Or anything else that your own instincts guide you to.

Clean Your House, Clear Your Psyche

One more point about cleaning your space. This work might bring up long-buried childhood fears and memories; in fact, that's part of its purpose. You may find yourself unaccountably crying or recalling distant events.

As you let go of the extraneous junk from your home, you may be releasing blocked energies from your body and psyche. It's all one. That's why it can feel so exhilarating to clear spaces. Some folks have literally *entombed* themselves with stuff in order to not feel. So, things are *meant* to emotionally come up in this process. Let it happen.

STEP 3: FILL YOUR MIND WITH THE POSITIVE

Hopefully, by now you've stopped saying stuff like, *This'll never change, I'll never have enough, I'm always broke*, or—one of the most rampant delusions ever—*Why does everyone always get whatever* they *want except me?*

For the remaining weeks, protect your gorgeous psyche from complaining about lack. Simply drop it for now.

If you catch yourself falling back into useless mental habits, don't worry. You might notice, *Okay, I'm back in the old saga again*, but that's common.

Instead, replace it with, "Miraculously, amazingly, everything I need always comes. God is opening me to receive beyond anything I imagine."

The Car Accident

When I began teaching the course, I was rear-ended hard at a red light by a hit-and-run driver. While my Prius was totaled, I was somehow fine. Though very shaken, I sure didn't waste any time wondering how I could have manifested such "terrible" luck. Instead, even as I sat breathless in the smashed car, I immediately offered the whole deal to God.

When I called the insurance company, Gary, the agent, asked whether I wanted to stay with the car or go home, but I could barely think straight. Half joking, I said I'd consult my mini-tarot deck in the glove compartment.

Imagine my surprise when Gary exclaimed, "Oh my gawd . . . tarot! Girl, *I* read cards too! What deck do you have? Crowley? And you got the Wheel of Fortune? Well, okay then, doll, we *both* know this is gonna work out just *fine*."

I felt like I was hallucinating. I mean, who knew Allstate had a secret tarot reader? No one could make this stuff up. As Gary and I talked, I felt my breathing return and my body eventually relax and let go.

Steve, my case adjuster, was also an angel. He got me the reimbursement check within four days, almost totally covering the new car. Then he said, "You know, I want to tell you, I've been doing this work forever and have seen *it all.* I'm convinced this came in record time because you weren't staying pissed at the drunk who hit you. Some people get so paralyzed by anger, they block the next phase. You'll be in a new car within a week."

He was right. Even better, the week before the accident, I'd been hounded by a company trying to sell me an expensive extended warranty to start at 75,000 miles. I kept saying no without knowing why. As they towed away the old car, I spied the odometer: 74,999.

God Chases You

You may even find that what you've been pursuing forever will begin to pursue you. A farmer in the course had one such wild experience.

For months, she'd tried with no luck to sell the turkeys on her land, which had been a massive headache. One day someone called who wanted them all—ironically, right after she'd cleared *years* of junk from her home. "Fantastic," she said. "But now I have to catch them. What a nightmare!"

So she offered it all over. Why wouldn't God be as good with turkeys as anything else?

And lo and behold, when she stepped outside, the turkeys began to chase *her* for the first time ever. Even while roaring with laughter, she quickly gathered them all.

This is indeed how it works. When you give everything to the Divine with detachment, things start to happen in a way that's the opposite of what we're taught.

In fact, here's one of the most beautiful surprises. By consistently following these steps, you actually build a love affair with Spirit. It's no longer a business transaction or a wish list, it's about Love.

Now, maybe you're thinking, *Wait a minute, I thought I was just reading this book to get my finances in order. What are you talking about Love for?* But listen, since everything else will be shifting for you anyway, you might as well throw this in too.

Invite the Divine to pursue you.

Seriously.

Just say, "I'm finally ready, God. Pursue me."

That's all.

Step 4: Gratitude Saves Your Buns

In India, gratitude is seen as one of the best ways to please Lakshmi, the beneficent multiarmed Goddess of Beauty and Prosperity.

They say if you're thankful for what you already have, She can't *help* but give you more. Though many beg Her for favors, it's far more powerful to just thank Her for your current good, no matter how seemingly small.

Twenty years ago, I was in a temple near Mumbai, fervently praying at Her statue for what felt like hours. When I finished, a man walked up and said, "Excuse me, madam. If it would be all right, may I trouble you with a question, please? To whom do you think you were praying? Do you not know that She is exactly You Yourself?"

Whoa! His words jolted me. I laughed and admitted I'd indeed completely forgotten. I remembered that the inner Divine is the highest, wisest part of ourselves. The Inner Lakshmi already *is* Abundance.

So you can pray to Her:

> *Fill me with gratitude for all You give. May I be a vehicle for You wherever I go. May I be grateful for every blessing and know Your abundance as my own Self. Open me to my own Inner Divinity and awaken me from the sleepwalk of being "only" human.*

Another way to appreciate Her is by treating the money you do have, no matter how little or much, with respect. She adores order and cleanliness, so the physical clearing of space we're doing is right up Her alley. But in Her honor, you can also clean your wallet, throwing out extraneous papers and stubs, and even organize all the bills by denomination. To some people this may sound extreme, but if you think about it, you're building a tiny portable temple for money.

Furthermore, gratitude can be shown by spending with awareness. You can respect what you *do* have, even if it's currently limited. Offering your finances never means burning through money recklessly and then saying, "Oh well, God's so infinite, She'll just bring more." Lakshmi rules honoring yourself as well as the Shakti of money. If you listen, your own intuition will show you where and where not to spend.

Finally, you can bless Her while you're paying the bills. Rather than curse the whole pile, you can say, "Thank God I have the money to pay these." And even if you currently don't, you can say, "Thank you that I soon will be able to pay!"

Step 5: Easy to Receive

For these weeks, let it be a mellifluous, steady chant in your head:

It's easy for me to receive.
It's easy for me to receive.
It's easy for me to receive.

Especially for women, reciting these words might be the single most revolutionary financial step you'll ever take. Many women (and some sensitive guys) are taught to incessantly overgive while simultaneously feeling unworthy to receive. A toxic fury burns inside: "I give and give, but when will my *own* damn turn come?" This resentment ironically blocks abundance of all kinds—not just money.

Saying *It's easy for me to receive* can shake your whole world in surprising ways.

While Danica was opening to this process, she dreamed one night that she was suffocating, unable to inhale. She woke up in a panic and saw she'd been giving without receiving her *entire* life. Her soul screamed, *You must inhale! You deserve to breathe and take up space. You are worthy.*

This statement can dislodge old anger, resentment, or bitterness. Some of these mental patterns have been passed to us from our ancestors through many lifetimes. Yet every time you affirm that you can receive, you move away from that inherited ancestral pain and toward a radiant opening.

Pupusa Dinner

As I walked to the store one night for groceries, I was chanting inside, *I'm open to receive, I'm open to receive.* I stood in front of the pupusa shop, wondering if I should buy one or save for groceries. Suddenly, I saw this homeless guy I used to give money to years ago.

He said, smiling, "Hey, I recognize you! I owe you ten dollars."

I was shocked. So I protested, "No, no, Jim, that's okay."

But he got out his wallet and insisted, "Yes, I must buy you dinner!"

Since I'd been repeating all day "I'm open to receive," how could I say no?

She was right. Once you say this, you don't dictate who or how. Besides, Jim may have needed to give her the money as much as she needed to receive it.

Let the Help Come

Sam, an acclaimed furniture maker, had been carrying a huge credit card debt for years, which filled him with embarrassment and remorse. He had lost his workspace and all his best pieces in an inferno in Los Angeles. When his wife left him at the same time, his spirit collapsed and hadn't recovered.

However, as he began to offer his unbearable calamity to the Divine, he had a singular, stunning thought, *Somehow, I will let Love do for me what I cannot do for myself.* The next day, an odd phone call came: His favorite aunt, a talented investor, had recently made a killing in Bitcoin. She'd hoped he wouldn't be offended, but she knew his situation and wanted to give him $20,000. As a gift, not a loan. Would he accept?

Amazingly, he was able to receive from her, fighting tears the whole way. In the past, he would have been far too humiliated to accept. But he knew his aunt was the conduit God had picked to get him back on his feet . . . and he was grateful.

The Pleasure of Receiving

Here's how it goes. You *deny* people the pleasure of giving when you're closed to receiving. In fact, you might be someone who needs to learn to *rein yourself in* from overgiving. If so, you can say, "Okay, God, I'm about to do it again. Let me relax, sit inside myself, and open to receive." For some people, "I deserve to receive" is the cosmic shift of many lifetimes.

Have you felt that rush of pleasure when someone is genuinely grateful for a gift you've given? Even if a present isn't to your taste, when you graciously receive it, you tell the Universe you are *open*. You honor the giver as a form of the Divine . . . and can always regift later.

As you continue to practice receiving, money from the past may return in some truly astonishing ways. For example, Beth got a note from an attorney saying, "I discovered that I charged you $1,500 more than I should have. Now, a year later, I'm compelled to return it." (Beth said she didn't want to reinforce tired stereotypes about lawyers, but if she ever needed a miracle to prove the existence of God, *this* was it.)

By opening to receive, past imbalances had room to be corrected. God had full permission to bring the money however He wanted—and indeed He did.

⊂HREE MORE TOOLS

Here are three easy ways to help open to Divine Source. Because the nature of this work is so practical, you can never have enough concrete ways to bring it down to earth.

GET A GOD BOX

Get a box, as fancy or simple as you like, to become the Divine container for your problems, longings, and fears around money (and anything else, for that matter). Whenever a burden comes up, write it down and stick the paper in the box, fully offering it. Ask for the right actions to be shown. If you continue to be anxious, remind yourself that the topic now belongs 100 percent to God since it's in the box. (By the way, this is perhaps the opposite of a vision board, since you're not telling the Universe *what* to do, but instead are casting the burden for a holy solution.)

This simple little box can be life-changing, as it makes offering a physical practice. Periodically, you can burn or throw out all the papers and start again. You may be surprised by how many issues have been resolved!

SMASH COCONUTS

The coconut can be the most unexpected and powerful tool for freeing your mind. The ritual is from India, but I've heard similar practices exist in the Caribbean and other spots. I like this exercise for any kind of big offering, but especially when you feel overwhelmed by something. I've broken so many of these over the years (and turned so many on to this practice) that I've jokingly wondered if there were any endorsement opportunities with Coconut Distributors of America.

The coconut represents the attachment of the mind to a particular problem and actually, if you look closely, it really does look like a head with two dark eyes and a mouth. You can usually find them at Asian markets or health food stores. One woman living in rural Wisconsin said she was so obsessed with getting one, she was thrilled to see she could order a package of three from Amazon.

So here's how to use them.

Get one with its hard, hairy shell intact. Make sure you can hear the milk sloshing inside. Sit and meditate with it, offering to God the whole burden you want to release. Then go smash the bejeesus out of it. I often say, "As I throw this, release me from my chains. Take my offering and free me from this. All belongs to You alone!"

I like to throw it hard against a sidewalk or rock since the release as it explodes is deeply satisfying. (I know some people break these with a hammer, but to me, half the power comes from actually throwing them.) If a certain topic has tortured you forever, you may even feel immediate freedom when the coconut breaks. I remember the first time I smashed one, a weight I'd carried since childhood was shattered to bits and never returned.

(Note: Do *not* save the pieces to eat. You just broke the symbolic container for your ancient, gnarly-ass problem, so throw it away.)

I prefer to do this ritual at a beach or park, but I've done it in all *kinds* of spots. You'll be guided. I once taught a class in L.A. where we trooped into a nearby alley for a riotous breaking ceremony. One woman got so enthusiastic that she accidentally pitched it hard over a high fence into someone's garden. A moment later the shocked owner stumbled out, carrying the whole broken mess. Thank god she wasn't hit. That was insane even for L.A.!

By the way, if you live somewhere where you simply can't get one just work with what you've got. Some people have used a melon, an egg, or an old dish. What matters is the pure intention of offering and release.

MAKE DEMOS OF ABUNDANCE

Here's the third tool. Act *as if* you're prosperous, even if you don't feel it yet. Perhaps you give somebody a big gratuity, especially if you've often thought in the past, *I don't tip much. Maybe I will if I'm rich one day.*

Instead, you start now.

You begin to let God use you to give.

Sometimes money literally has to have permission to go in one hand and out the other.

But don't misunderstand me. Some people rip through money compulsively to hide deep feelings of emptiness, but this isn't about reckless spending. Instead, I'm talking about making a demonstration of abundance as a demonstration of *faith.*

As you give to others, you feel: *It's easy for me to spend God's money to help.*

Tithing is a reliable way to do this. You take 10 percent of "your" money and demonstrate *This is* really *not mine.* (Now, I might argue that *none* of it actually is, but you know what I mean.) When you tithe, you're saying, *Ten percent is God's. I'll give back wherever I'm shown.*

By the way, a tithe need not only go to what spiritually sustains you. Some people give to political, environmental, or animal groups, or to a friend in need, women's shelters—anywhere that's important to them. Your own heart will show. If this is hard, you can pray, "Let a miracle happen and help me give back."

Even if you have little or are temporarily financially restricted, this can open the conduit—if you do so without a grudge. Even a small amount of giving can open the flow.

"Use me, God, so Your money can pass through me to those who need."

Someone in the course pointed out that you could tithe in ways other than money, such as volunteering. And while I don't want to diminish the power of that, here's what I've seen: Some people offer time generously but still think, *Sure, I'll volunteer, but when we get to the coins, they're* all *mine.* For some people, the dollars and cents themselves have to be given. Then tithing can bring the experience: I give this on behalf of Love.

Even giving $10 while the mind protests, *No, it's mine. I'm scared.* can be transformative. You start to feel that it's safe to give. You rest in Divine Source. You open to a life where there's enough time, money, and love.

I once heard a minister say that when she wasn't giving enough, God just took it anyway. She might have thought, *I want to donate to the homeless fund,* but then wouldn't, to save for an emergency.

Invariably, a crisis would indeed come, for the exact amount she'd wanted to donate. Her car battery would die, her dog would get sick, or she'd crack a filling. So she started to give when prompted, knowing that Love would take Its share regardless. It was so much easier to cooperate!

GUILT OVER GOOD FORTUNE

Tithing is great medicine if you tend to feel guilty for any good fortune you're experiencing. Rather than feeling bad, you offer some straight back to Love. Then you're actually being a helpful conduit rather than thinking, *Who am I to have this?* You give full permission to be Divinely and effectively used on the planet for the good.

A Meditation for Giving Freely

Take a moment to focus inside. Let your body settle. Feel your mind grow quiet.

Then imagine a waterfall of light pouring through the top of your head.

Hold your hands open, and as that waterfall streams through you, allow it to pour out of your hands. Feel it as a natural flow of light that wants to come through you and out into the world.

Imagine that this light then swirls back upward and in again through the crown of your head. Let it form a circular pattern as it comes from your hands and passes through the top of your head and back through your hands.

Just imagine yourself part of this radiant waterfall of light. Know that financial abundance and prosperity are part of this—they're not separate. The more you see yourself as a vehicle for giving and receiving, the more everything that wants to come can come, and everything that wants to go can go.

Hold your hands wide open to receive and wide open to give. Let it be easy. Feel it as a relief. You don't have to cling to it all. You don't have to fear. You're a container for giving and receiving.

Slowly come back out. And just hold this simple image: You yourself are a waterfall of abundance, even if you don't see it in your bank account yet. It doesn't matter. See it coming in; see it going out. You're part of that waterfall of light.

FAREWELL TO THE STORY

As you use all these tools, you may find that financial "stories" you've been telling yourself forever will start to dissipate. In fact, these outworn tales can be offered directly to Love. They can be written down and put into the God Box or mentally placed in a coconut and then smashed. You can even pray, "Make me ready to release this!"

Sometimes stories such as "I'm always a victim" or "God always punishes me" have served an emotional purpose in your past, or at least have been familiar to the inner kid. But you can begin to say, *It's okay, honey, we're no longer trapped in childhood anymore. This life now belongs to Love, and anything can happen!*

RELEASING SELF-TORTURE

Many people blame themselves daily for certain "financial mistakes" from the past, but as you offer to the Divine, you may lose your passion for this as well. For example, you stop berating yourself for not locking your car the day it was stolen 10 years ago. Instead, you can say: "Let me forgive myself. May I trust that every loss can be replaced as I open to Your abundance."

As the weight of these traumatic events starts to lighten, beating yourself up can even become boring. *Do I really have to go down that same pothole-filled road again? May I offer all back to Love to be shown the way.*

You can say, "Please show me how to treat myself kindly about this." For example, let's say you're still blaming yourself for a bad investment. That festering ire can definitely block the good that wants to come in the present. But as you forgive yourself, you open once again to the Divine Flow, where any loss can potentially be followed by gain.

Besides, is there a person alive who hasn't made money errors? What a relief to say, "Okay, God, You know what occurred. But I'm handing You all regrets since You alone are my Source."

So don't waste this precious life beating yourself up for the past. Just move straight to offering. You may feel Love comforting you, whispering, *Now we share this burden. The right actions will be shown.*

I was thinking the other day about Jesus's famous line "Father, forgive them, for they know not what they do" (Luke 23:34). But what if it was also used inside ourselves? Many of us persecute ourselves for money mistakes made when we just didn't know better.

So a prayer could be, "May I forgive myself; I knew not what I did." When Divine Source is invoked and the channel for abundance is opened, you never know what the Universe may bring.

My good friend Dan had persecuted himself forever for not buying into the insane Bay Area real estate market. "I obsess about it so much," he confessed, "I can even start hyperventilating. I could have gotten that cute cottage on Elmwood ten years ago for five hundred K. I still follow it on Zillow like a stalker, and now it's one point five mil. What an idiot!"

I laughed and rolled my eyes. "Don't you remember? You had great reasons for not buying back then. Anyway, if you were meant to buy it, you *would* have. What if it simply wasn't meant to be?"

Every day, Dan sat in a firepit of self-blame with so much tsuris and regret, no other home had room to come. I suggested that since he was already bereft, he had nothing to lose by praying, "Let me forgive myself completely. I knew not what I did."

I was honestly shocked when Dan agreed. As he let go, for the first time in years he noticed other potential properties.

This prayer works in tandem with Divine Selection, which says no individual person, place, or thing is your Source, only God. There's no need to fret about the one that got away. When God is reinstalled as the storehouse of all, there's no tragically missed opportunity. Only a move into the present, where what's meant to be yours will always come.

Meditation on Financial Regrets

Go inside for a moment. Just focus on your breath. Feel your body and your mind settle and grow quiet.

Feel this connection to this inner light, this inner Divine—however you imagine this presence. Then let it show you something that still brings up resentment from your own financial past. You may be blaming yourself for this, or you may be blaming somebody else. Just notice the very first thing that comes up, without any judgment.

Then imagine you can take it, whatever it is, and offer it completely to that waterfall of light.

Say, "Wash it away. Free me from the illusion that this is my Source. Let me forgive myself; let me forgive anyone else. Let me forgive whatever is needed. I no longer want to be ruled by this. Divine abundance itself is my Source. I can forgive the past. I've learned what I needed to learn from this, and I'm ready to release it. If there are any actions I still need to take, show me them. Prepare me to release this."

Then let another thing come up: another issue, person, way of blaming yourself, or something else you haven't been able to let go of—another illusion created in your mind about not having enough. Take that issue and offer it up to that radiant waterfall. Say, "I'm ready. I don't want to be held captive by this anymore. The Divine itself is my Source for everything. Let me forgive myself. Let me forgive the other person. If there's any action to take, show me. Otherwise, set me free."

Deepening

And then, as you're ready, slowly come back out. Bring this awareness with you—this feeling that whatever those two issues are, they now belong to God. If they start to come up again, if you start to resent yourself again, if you catch yourself blaming yourself again . . . just offer them back.

ENERGETIC CLEARING

*Wanna fly, you got to give up the shit
that weighs you down.*

— Toni Morrison, *Song of Solomon*

In Weeks Two and Three, we focused on the external side of saucha, clearing the home to make it a container for abundance. In Week Four, we move to the other part of saucha, clearing the internal energy. But before we do this, let's dive a bit more into house clearing.

CLEANING VERSUS NEAT FREAK

One topic that often confuses people is the difference between cleaning and neatness. Offering all your belongings to Love is different from having to be tidy.

> I understand releasing stuff, it's important. But I must tell you, I'm annoyed, 'cause I'm not actually a tidy person. I think, Tosha, maybe you're just a neat freak convincing us all to have these super Zen spaces. Sometimes I like that, but often I prefer a mess.

Okay, I totally hear you.

I'll admit, I'm a highly visual person who even gets anxious around dirty dishes. (Yep, I wash them right after dinner because waking up to them the next day can fill me with a nearly existential dread.) But that's not the point.

I respect that some folks are neat and others are not. What matters is purging the stuck and obstructive energy of the things you no longer *love, use, or need.* A friend who's a former teacher told me that despite being orderly by nature, she couldn't believe the mountains of old files she'd cleared during this process. That's common.

As you winnow, you may feel the energy shifting around you (and within you). In Chinese medicine, it's believed that "stagnant chi" needs to be reanimated. This happens in homes as well.

Once you've cleared and cleared, how you handle what remains is totally up to you. If you want to take what's left and make one wild pigpen of it all, well, darlin', have at it! As long as we don't have to live together, I support you all the way.

Burning My Journals

Many years ago, in the midst of clearing my apartment, I felt guided to torch most of my journals. Yet I wondered, *Am I crazy? How can I do this? I'm a* writer. *What if I want to write a memoir down the road?*

But here's the truth. When I read the journals—mostly from my torturous twenties—I knew they were useless. They were volume after volume of confusion, fear, and complaints. Besides, as organized as I can be, my penmanship was (and still is) like a deranged pharmacist's, semi-illegible even to me. Burning that pile of self-hatred was a powerful way to release a persona I could barely recall. As they smoldered in the fireplace, my heart danced as page after page surrendered to the orange flames.

I've never regretted it, but I wouldn't say that *you* should have to do this, too, since everyone's different. Your own journals might be so great, you're the next Annie Dillard or Colette. Like everything else, if you offer it to the Divine, *you will be shown.*

Inner Knowing Leads

Okay, now that your home is on the way to being a temple, let's focus on your inner energy. You'll do this primarily by removing unneeded psychic cords, which are energy ropes that bind us to pivotal people and things.

As you enter this inner realm, continue to honor your instincts. You're probably getting more comfortable following the spanda as you clear your home, and you can apply that skill within yourself as well.

The more you offer, the more you're able to "hear" within and the less you may care about one-size-fits-all rules. You start to get shown what's needed from the *inside*. I encourage you to continue adjusting these practices to fit your own psyche.

In fact, the more you offer, the more you start to trust . . . *you*. I'll give you guidelines, but your own authority led by the inner Divine will blossom. By the end of this process, that quiet Knowing will hopefully be stronger than ever.

ENDING THE INNER WAR

My friend Carlotta is so nervous about everything she eats, she trots through the health food store with her wooden pendulum, testing each cauliflower head or carob bar with a vengeance. As someone with a sensitive body, I understand that. On the other hand, Carlotta constantly tells herself the most tragic and belittling things, beating herself with a mental bat from morning to night.

To me, the terrible things we tell ourselves can have a toxicity *far beyond* what we consume. Over time, through offering and clearing, the war inside can cease.

This is a regime change that can only happen from within. The inner despot of harshness and self-blame is slowly deposed, forever freeing you from its reign of terror. A softer, more forgiving way is en route.

CORDS AND CHAKRAS

Ironically, many of the financial beliefs that tyrannize us are not even our own. For example, we might hold some that our mom felt while we were in utero. We absorb these through a kind of osmosis, and they form psychic cords that hold us captive. These "ties that bind" can leave us feeling entangled and powerless.

These truly can feel like psychic lassos. Certain attitudes about money, such as *I'll never have enough*, may simply be cords to a spouse or parent. For example, if your father had one financial crisis after another, you might expect your own pattern will be the same. But taking off his cord might restore you to sanity, or at least to your *own* destiny, so you don't feel you must relive *his*.

Usually cords have not been attached with diabolical intentions, though, of course, occasionally they have. Often it was just the other person's limiting belief or wound that got stored within you like a parasite.

The great news is that these sticky ropes can be removed. We'll be clearing them in the same way you would a messy room, and then we'll ground you back in the present, in your *own* sacred relationship to Divine Source.

But first we need to talk about chakras, the energy centers located along the spine, since that's where the cords attach. We have (at least) seven of them, with the first at the base of the spine and the last at the crown. For the purposes of our process, we'll focus mostly on the lower three centers, all of which relate to security. In general, I've found that's where the most virulent cords fasten.

You might have someone hooked into the grounding chakra at the base of the spine, or the second chakra, the survival and creativity center right below your navel. Or attached to the power chakra at your solar plexus. Or perhaps to all three. With a little practice, you'll be able to sense which chakras are hooked to someone else's wounds and fears, or even to a past life.

Alix was corded to the horrible trauma of her father's suicide, which happened when she was 10. Although she'd had years of therapy, she still often felt as if she were frozen in that event. After a few repetitions of the meditation we're about to do, she was able to cut the cord to her father at her second chakra and finally stand on her own feet. The release freed her to fully be in the present.

Now, you needn't be paranoid about cords, because once you're aware of them, they're actually not hard to remove. Though clearing can be done around any type of issue, we'll focus here specifically on finances. This meditation will guide you.

Cord Meditation

I hope you'll do this a number of times during the remaining weeks. You'll probably have more than one person or event come up, but notice what central one presents itself first:

Focus on your breath and allow your energy to drop inside. Feel as if the earth is supporting you and your mind quieting.

Allow yourself to sense, bubbling up into your being, somebody that you're corded to about money. It could be a partner, or a parent; it could be someone from your past—anyone whose views about money you've been storing in your body.

You may even notice where you've been storing this. You may see the rope attaching below your belly button or to the base of your spine. You may see it attaching to your power center, in your solar plexus. Trust what you're getting. Just take the first person that comes.

Then say to them, "We're complete now. I'm reowning my connection to God's money. I have my own holy connection to it, and I reown this fully, because I deserve to live from a state of abundance. I deserve to trust that I will have enough. I deserve the good. I deserve to be a vehicle for abundance.

"I'm now removing this cord. I'm removing this rope to you from my own body."

Take it off in a way that's easiest for you. You might pull, burn, or cut it off.

You can thank that person; you can even wish them all the highest blessings. You can say, "We are complete. This cord is no longer running my system. I will now have my own relationship to God's largesse. I am free to be a vehicle for God's good."

Whoever you found on this first round is central. That's why they came up. Just taking off that one attachment may make you feel more present in your own body. You'll be starting your own relationship to the Divine's money rather than living theirs.

Now, let yourself drop in again. You're just going to see one image. It could be an event from this lifetime, or it could be from a past life. Your psyche will show you one event from the past that you're corded to—one that's keeping you in a place of fear or scarcity. If you're getting many pictures, that's fine; just take the first one that comes and then return to the others later, using this same technique.

This primary image could be something that happened, or something you're scared of, or even a memory. Let it come up and play out, whatever it is. Once again, just feel the rope of energy that attaches you to that image. It will dissolve when you finally cut that cord or burn it away and say, "This memory is no longer my reality. The power of God is stronger than this dream." Just feel yourself releasing it, as if you're watching a balloon fly away in the sky. See it leave. It no longer determines what's possible. It's no longer your story. You've cut the cord and made space for Love to bring what's needed.

Feel the release of the cord to that central person and image. If they ever try to reattach, you can swat them away. You're no longer available.

And then, take a final moment back in your own body to say, "It's easy for me to receive. It's easy to receive the highest Divine plan and become a vehicle for the good."

Then, when you're ready, slowly come back out, remembering all that occurred.

RECLAIMING THE POWER

For some of you, one cord meditation might be enough to clear the dominant person blocking the way. But others may find a veritable crowd in the lower three chakras—several people whose beliefs about money still trap you. It doesn't matter. Just go back each day and continue to clear for as long as you need. After you do this, it can help to drink plentiful water and rest, if needed.

Keep in mind that no cord can stay attached without your *permission*. The first step is simply to become aware. Once you get in the practice of detecting them, they become much more obvious. You won't even necessarily have to be in meditation.

For example, on a hard day, you might be walking around thinking—yet again—that you'll never, ever have enough. Then suddenly you sense a tugging at your second chakra. Maybe you even see a fleeting image of your sister. Out of the blue, you have the awareness: *Wow, I've always been carrying her fear here. We were so close I picked it all up.*

And you pluck it off.

Please be gentle as you remove these, especially in the beginning. While it's a straightforward process, you may feel a little tired or spaced out at first. After all, someone's psychic energy may have hooked you forever, and now you're saying, "No more. Party over!" But don't forget, cords are a natural phenomenon, and you're simply reclaiming your own energy. You can even send the other people love, blessings, or appreciation while you make the separation.

As you become increasingly aware and present, you address each cord with patience and love. You pluck them off as you find them. With a little practice, it just becomes second nature. No big deal. They may occasionally return, but don't fret. For example, one day, you might find yourself in a wave of financial fear, but then quickly realize, *Wow, I'm hooked again. I retapped my family's terror, but since it's not mine, I gratefully release it.*

With these tools, you're no longer at the mercy of scarcity thoughts. Over time, you'll make the decision to align with *truth* instead of falsehoods. Lies like "I'll never get what I need. I can never receive. I'll always be envious" will lose their power. You'll simply notice when you slip into old patterns, and you'll gratefully return to the truth.

The Full Abundance Change Me Prayer says it all.

> *Change me into one who can fully love, forgive, and accept myself so I may carry Your Light without restriction. Let everything that needs to go, go. Let everything that needs to come, come.*
>
> *I am utterly Your own.*

Some Examples

Cords may affect you physically in surprising ways you never could have imagined. Cutting them can sometimes bring intense relief.

This is so powerful! I've cut cords many times before, but never like this.

My uncle came to live with us when I was about nine, and soon after I began to have terrible lower-back pain. No medical test could explain why. So today, when I saw who was corded to me, of course it was my uncle. The rope ran from the front of my pelvis, through my perineum, and onto my lower back. The pain was fiery hot.

I cut it, releasing my uncle's deep sense of scarcity, and lo and behold, away went my pain! I never would've put the two together if I hadn't experienced this firsthand.

De-cording can also help release fear coming through generations of suffering. It's common to hold someone from your childhood in one of the lower three centers and then re-create their anxieties in your own life.

My Chinese mother grew up the youngest of eight, with four kids in one bed and another four scattered throughout the apartment. Her father died when she was little, and my grandmother, who spoke no English, was left to care for them all. They all grew up hungry and scared. Yet I'm finding as I release these cords to both my mother and grandmother, I'm regaining my own sense of power in all areas, including money. I feel enormous compassion for what they experienced, but know I'm learning a different way to be that grows stronger each day.

Some of this cord removal is just downright funny. This makes me laugh.

I just did the cord-cutting meditation for the first time. The person I released was my ex-husband, who's actually still a good friend. I had a long-standing debt to him that I'd been paying back since our divorce four years ago, but your course convinced me to clean up the rest. So it seemed fitting to cut the cord.

But check this out. Right after I finished, I opened Facebook to see that he had changed his cover photo. There had been a picture of the two of us, but now he'd cropped me out! At first I was insulted, until I saw he'd done it precisely during the meditation. Whoa!

Yes indeed, someone intuitive may sense you've uncorded them. You may still adore them and be close, but you won't be tied in a way that limits your freedom and clarity.

Knowing how to remove cords is like possessing a sacred sword in your bag of tricks. Even so, you may occasionally find you need help getting the "stickiest" ones to stay off. When that happens, you can always call in a form like Archangel Michael with his saber of light to do the dirty work. Lord Ganesh, the remover of obstacles, or Kali, the Goddess of Death and Rebirth, can equally pulverize these ropes. If you need the help, feel free to invite it.

Past lives

Maybe you grew up in a family where there *was* enough, yet you still freak out often about money. I was puzzled by this myself until I began to ponder past lives. When you extend the range of influence beyond the current incarnation, many things make sense, including questions like, "How could Mozart have composed a complete piano concerto at age five?" or "How could Joan of Arc have led that army as a mere teenager?"

So, it's not only talent and abilities that get carried over; many fears and phobias, including those about money, can emanate from the memories and impressions of these past lifetimes. Perhaps in another era you died in the bubonic plague in Europe or lost everything in an earthquake in Tibet. You never know.

Or maybe you *do.*

Someone once led me on a past-life regression where I saw with crystalline clarity a lifetime during the Edo period in Kyoto, Japan, where I'd been a struggling geisha. The vision was so vivid, I felt the fear as if it were yesterday. While some Westerners might imagine a rarified life of exquisite food and kimonos, I felt constant financial desperation amidst the beauty. To survive, I was totally at the mercy of finding a generous *danna*, or patron, who would subsidize my food and clothing.

I realized that the financial worries that had dogged me the first half of this life came in part from those Edo days. It also explained why I'd always felt profoundly at home around Japanese aesthetics and culture.

ABOUT SACRIFICE AND LOSS

In a sense, you could say you learn how to offer through disappointment and loss. True offering is a passionate and direct invitation for Love to take over and bring Her own plan instead of the ego's.

And sometimes, here's the truth, it's just unbearably painful. You feel as if She's cutting away all that needs to go: illusions, obsessions, addictions . . . often without an anesthetic.

This is why I adore viewing everything as a sacrifice to Love.

In India, Vedic priests do gorgeous *yagnas*, or holy fire ceremonies, where they make prayers to the presiding deities, such as Lakshmi, Kali, and Ganesh. At different junctures, ghee, milk, rice, turmeric, and colorful flowers are fed to the fire. Rather than only casting your problem to the Divine, you're giving something back as well.

Life can be seen the same way.

A friend of mine was in Argentina a few years ago when someone walked up and yanked a cherished necklace off her neck. Understandably she was badly shaken. But when she told me, I couldn't help saying, "You know, you're at a massive turning point in your life right now. You're leaving behind so much that you no longer need. Maybe Kali just took a sacrifice for the new time and it's all one crazy blessing. Who *knows* what She may bring instead?"

I didn't know how my friend might answer. But she shuddered in recognition and became immediately relieved about the "loss."

Even in the greatest catastrophes, these ideas of offering and sacrifice can bring enormous consolation and help.

I'm one of the many who lost a home in the Northern California fires. I'm also one of the businesspeople here who lost most of our income because our clients were affected as well. Yet somehow, I've been financially carried. It was a miracle we got FEMA and a couple of grants. Then our friends started a benefit page and we got a low-interest business loan to help us rebuild.

But even with all these gifts, I've felt terrified and bewildered. Now I realize it's more about losing an ego construct . . . who I thought I was.

So I thank you for the concept of sacrifice. If I can view the devastation as that and bless it, I feel full instead of empty. If the catastrophe can be a sacrifice, then I know I'm part of Something Bigger. Having gone through all of this, I love the reminder to let Divine abundance to come through me as opposed to thinking everything is mine.

Releasing money fears

For this last section on releasing money fears, let me share a few letters from people going through this particular week of the process. You may find comparable issues happening for you.

The Computer Debacle

My son spilled water on my brand-new MacBook, and the next morning, when I turned it on, it wouldn't turn off. Total panic.

When I took it to Apple, they said it was probably the motherboard and they'd let me know. It could cost nothing . . . or $800.

For the first time in my life, I decided to totally offer it to God, and whatever the outcome, I'd be fine. Every time worry arrived, I reminded myself that it was God's. Imagine my excitement when four days later they said it would cost nothing. Thank you so much for helping us think this way!

This next one is about offering even while you're waiting for things to line up.

RESTING IN THE MIDDLE

Here's what's nuts. I've done all the steps every day, and though I keep running out of money, new opportunities keep appearing! I feel more peaceful than I have in years.

I've never in my life experienced ease with money. For me to currently have little and yet still feel relaxed is unbelievable. I'm learning how to just be "in the middle," when the shift is occurring, but I'm not yet on the other side.

You may be experiencing something similar. You may get tested at times, when money *has* to keep flowing out no matter *what* you do. It may come in and go straight back out. Don't panic. The Universe could simply be getting you comfortable with being a conduit. Later, the money can accumulate.

Okay, one more about financial fears.

MISTAKES WERE MADE

Recently, the accounting for my home business got screwed up, and I prayed for help, knowing this could finally heal my money anxieties. I found myself asking for protection so this wouldn't be discovered.

But I love your approach where we don't regard money as our own. If the money isn't mine, why would I need to pray for protection? Is it only important to forgive myself for the mistake?

Offering deftly moves the consciousness from "This terrible thing happened. Please hide it!" to, "I give this to You. May the right actions be shown." You feel the difference.

You can offer a mistake fully and say, "Okay, God, You know what occurred. You're the provider of all. I'm handing You every single fear about this error. May all happen for the Highest according to Your Will."

And yes, you're right. You can never, ever go wrong with forgiving yourself . . . or anyone else for that matter.

WHEN NOTHING'S HAPPENING

Perhaps at the end of this week some of you might say, *Well, I'm using the tools and hearing these amazing stories, but nothing much is happening for* me *yet. What am I doing wrong?*

Nothing. *Just relax and continue the steps.*

If you feel the need to do more, go deeper into offering. Find another corner of your house to clear. Maybe do another cording meditation. Continue to repeat the Full Abundance Change Me Prayer and say, "It's easy for me to receive." Make a demonstration or two of abundance, set up a God Box, or break a coconut.

Some people are so attached to the idea that they're doing something wrong that they feel this no matter *what.* They gaze around, thinking, "Oh, man, *everyone* else has got this right. Why can't I?"

Just bless and release all that.

A part of the Law of Divine Selection is Divine timing. It means that all delays are beneficial, whether we see it or not. As you relax into opening, things will come together at the right time with surprising ease because it's all on God's clock.

Each of you will move through this process at your own rate because you're on a unique and sacred road mapped by the intelligence of your own soul. For some of you, these first weeks may have brought the relief of a quieter mind and a cleaner home. But beyond that, you may not know.

But then—and I've seen this again and again—suddenly, two or three months later, *wham*. A *massive* shift can come from seemingly nowhere . . . because you're ready. You bloom in your own time. So stay focused in right this moment. You're building a container for abundance.

For today, just these two questions are enough: What are you guided to clean out? And what are you releasing?

WEEK FIVE

The Forgotten Inner Kid

"Adults" . . . is a word that means obsolete children.

— Dr. Seuss

In Week Five, as you continue to do the steps and cut cords, we're going to address a critical, often-neglected piece of the abundance story: your inner child. We'll connect deeply with it because it's often the source of many, many financial fears.

HEARING THE CHILD

Claude was grateful he had a materially generous family growing up. But what he really wanted was somebody—anybody—to look him in the eye and say, "Tell me what happened today; I'd love to know how you feel. I've got all the time in the *world* for you." It had never happened as a kid, and as he grew older, he found it hard to believe it ever would.

Eventually, he saw that he could either stay mad about the situation, which many people do (they're 40 and incensed about events from age 3), or he *himself* could start to give that kid what it needed. To his surprise, Claude discovered that his inner child was thrilled to receive love and attention!

In the end, you're the one. You're the savior. No matter who you are, your own inner little one is waiting for *you*.

Like Claude, I, too, often felt I wasn't heard when I was little. I've learned to say to that shy and lonely girl, *Tell me everything. I'll listen for as long as you want. I'm not leaving, and I'm not in a hurry.* Those are still her favorite words in the world: *I'll listen as long as you want. Take your time.*

In our caffeinated world of multitasking madness, how many people will sincerely say that to you? "Take as long as you need. I'll give you my rapt attention." Even partners who love each other often try to catch up quickly while doing 14 other things.

Giving someone your complete presence is an astonishing gift. And what a treat to give that to your own inner kid. Sometimes mine has wanted me to write down every single thing she says, as if I'm taking dictation. I've found this much more critical to our relationship than buying her stuff.

I do love beautiful objects, but when someone has a shopping compulsion (or any other obsession, for that matter), usually a deeper hunger lurks underneath. It won't be solved by spanking or berating yourself. By communing with that kid, you'll eventually become her greatest ally.

Meditation for Communing

First, shake out your hands and fingers. Shake out your legs. Shake out your energy. Let go of anything from the day, then bring the energy back inside.

Focus on your breath and feel your body settle. Allow yourself to relax on the earth. Feel your mind quiet.

Imagine a force of love in your heart. You may see a deity, a goddess, or just the light, but feel it inside as your own Great Self. Even when you forget, its love remains. It's always there.

Then, invite that young child into your heart. Notice its age. It may be 3, it may be 6, or 10. Or even older.

Allow it to enter. Let it know that you're going to do a little meditation so it can start to feel heard and seen. You really want to give it your full attention.

For some of you, it may feel like a feral kitten who's been in a closet for a long time and is very reticent. For others, it'll just jump out there and you'll see it right away. It may be shy, or it may be playful and boisterous.

Just feel that you're its sacred caretaker and what a great honor to finally give it the time and attention it craves.

It'll tell you now, or convey somehow, what it wants from you in this moment. It may want to crawl into your lap and cuddle. It may want to talk, or it may just want to sit there and look at you. It'll let you know.

Let it tell you: Is it scared of anything right now? What's going on? Give it room to tell you, without any judgment or condescension. You're just listening. Maybe you're holding it. Let it tell you its fears.

And feel that you're allowing a wise, clear part of yourself to comfort and reassure this kid. You're letting it know especially that all finances are now offered to the Divine; you're learning a different way to be. You're letting it know that you'll be taking care of it from this point on, listening, comforting.

And all needs will be met.

Take a few moments and just be in that. If you need to say more—it may be distrustful or not so sure about you—reassure it that from now on, in communion with the Divine, you'll be present. Let it know that whatever it feels right now is fine.

It may even show a grudge from childhood or something more recent. It may even be mad at you for vanishing all these years! See if there's something it resents. Hear it out and let it know all feelings are fine, but a different time is arriving, where its needs will finally be met. You may have to apologize for being "gone" for so long!

Whatever comes up, reassure it that you've turned a new corner and are committed. But it can take as long as it needs to trust you. There's no hurry. And let it know especially that all finances will now be in the hands of your wise Self, so it won't have to fret about them.

Make one promise to it that you'll keep: whatever it wants, small or big.

And then, when you're ready, slowly come back out. Take a couple moments to write down what happened.

BEFRIENDING THAT CHILD

For some people, life can feel like a daily tantrum, all coming from that poor neglected young one. This affects not only money, but every part of life. When you look inside, you'll often see that the one who's enraged, lonely, or hopeless isn't even the adult part of you. It's that abandoned one inside crying for love. How things change when you begin to care for it!

My inner kid often feels like a martyr about money, just as my mom did. How can I best address this?

First, the cord to the mother needs to be removed so that her emotional pattern isn't re-created. Then the connection to that martyred child can be healed and strengthened. You can reassure it that it deserves to have needs and you'll help it say no. Every martyr needs to learn healthy boundaries.

You learn over time to stop identifying as that persecuted little kid who's alternating between helplessness and fury, and you become the loving adult caring for it. With practice, you really can become its compassionate guardian.

This guardianship unfolds organically like a flower, and after a while you'll be amazed by how your emotions shift. The child will begin to feel heard, and eventually it won't constantly squall for attention. Even if you find that after years of neglect, your inner kid has given up and sits in a state of numb abandonment, don't worry. No situation is hopeless. The Divine can work with anything!

The idea of the inner kid is nothing new; many therapists and healing modalities have addressed it for decades, going back to Carl Jung and John Bradshaw. But it's one thing to intellectually know *I have this little one inside who wants attention* and entirely another to fully commit to caring for it.

Many people treat that young one with impatient annoyance: *Why don't you just grow up? What's wrong with you? Get it together!* Often, they'll parrot how they were spoken to growing up. But there's another way: treat it with patience and love.

This is a learnable skill, especially with Divine help. If the child isn't getting the love from *you* that it's crying for, no amount of *outer* attention or coddling will ever do. Even the greatest partner or best friend can only supplement what you give inside. The first line of defense for that tender, waiting child is you.

And it isn't about repressing it, stifling it, or telling it to buck up and stop being a baby.

It's about inner kindness and compassion.

THE KID IS A SHOPAHOLIC!

As you become an ally to this young one, you'll recognize how it acts out when it's scared or lonely. Overspending can be one of many ways.

> A part of me constantly wants to buy clothes and accessories, yet if I never bought another such thing ever again, I'd still have plenty. It's out of control! How do I rein it in?

Your inner child is running the show by buying all these clothes and accessories just to soothe herself. Instead, when she starts clamoring, you can say, *Yes, we'll buy a bit, but I want to start to give you time and attention as well.* She'll eventually stop trying to fill the void in the old way.

Rather than spank or punish her, it's powerful to talk with her and negotiate. A loving parent probably wouldn't tell a five-year-old, "Hey, go run in that store and just buy the whole joint! Meet ya at the register." Instead, they might say, "Find one or two things you really love." Most kids actually thrive from a caring boundary.

If she's been neglected forever, she might say, *Why can't I have it all? I'm sure not getting any love or care from you, so gimme a hundred things instead!* Helping her feel safe and heard makes all the difference.

I'm spending more than I'm taking in, and it's not sustainable. I'm desperate to change from a fear-based child to a mature adult in my approach to finances.

I feel a huge sense of deprivation whenever I think of not getting what I want. If I successfully don't spend for a while, it just sets me up for a spending binge. And then I go into a terror about not being able to change my behavior.

I'm so tired of having this issue and oscillating between intense shame and panic.

How do I stop beating myself up for all the terrible financial habits I've indulged in?

It's actually common for the kid to have made disastrous financial decisions. It happens a lot! The first step is forgiveness. It's so powerful to say, *Listen, I want to forgive you for the past since you're really just a child. You were scared. How could you have known better? But from now on, God and I will be handling the money.* If you find it's impossible to stop blaming her, you can also *pray for the ability*.

That's the beauty of Divine Source. Losses can be followed by gains when you know that God is the origin and owner of all. You can stop beating the kid about money lost 20 years ago. Instead, you can think, *All right, what's done is done. Now, I'm finally learning how to care for the child* and *offer* all *finances to God for resolution.*

CARING FOR THE LITTLE ONE

For some people, just the idea of beginning to take tender care of the kid is formidable. A Change Me prayer can help: "Dear God, show me the first step to loving it. Make me ready!"

Olga admitted that she felt total revulsion for the task. She was infuriated that she had to learn to take care of that soft, vulnerable side. Why couldn't *someone else* come along and do it instead?

But the outside mirrors what's within. Until she was willing to reclaim and care for this abandoned part, *no one else could.* I suggested that rather than blame herself for being mad, she get the anger out physically by exercising or breaking something. For Olga, this was the first step to a loving inner connection.

Actually, one of the greatest surprises can be how inner tenderness and love for the child can be a consummate doorway to the Divine. Many people would say, "I don't have a connection to God, I've felt abandoned and bereft forever." And I'd answer, "Don't worry about that right now. Just focus on that kid and take care of it."

And then the damnedest miracle would occur.

They'd soon recognize that the unconditional love and forgiveness they poured to that neglected kid was actually coming direct from the inner Lord. The child was a fast and powerful path to union.

YOUR INNER DOG

If, for whatever reason, you can't relate to the idea of the inner child, you might want to try this tool instead.

> When you were talking about taking care of the kid, I realized just how much resistance I have to inner-child work. . . . What I just started doing instead is working with my inner animal, or what I've come to refer to as the Stray Dog of My Heart.
>
> I found myself, very clearly, with this stray who just showed up needing food, water, and a comfy bed by the fire. I saw how easily and lovingly I wanted to provide these things. He needed to be praised for his loyalty and bravery, for protecting me, protecting the house. He needed a job to do, to know what his boundaries are, and to know that he's safe and loved and belongs. I tell him what a good boy he is and that he's not abandoned anymore.
>
> Thank you, inner dog! Thank you for protecting me!

Maybe it's no funny accident that *dog* is the anagram for *God*. For some people, connecting to an inner animal of any kind comes more freely than connecting to the child. (Or it's an initial step before the kid comes forward.) Especially if you have a history of being brutal with yourself, imagining a pet within that you love and care for can create a massive shift. People will often freely give unconditional acceptance to an animal that they'd never normally give themselves.

Years ago, Maurice was a marathon runner who abused himself mercilessly whenever he got injured. He was truly incapable of taking a break to let his injuries heal. But as an animal lover, this idea of the inner pet really hit deeply. He knew he'd never beat his own beloved corgi for getting sick, but instead coddle him till he recovered. He saw that his own inner puppy deserved the same.

ᛒRINGING DOWN THE WALL

When contacted, some inner kids will run to you right away, excited to play, commune, and be noticed. But just as many will be rightfully furious for all the years of being hurt or ignored. In such cases, a patient period of reconciliation has to occur.

Some have felt abandoned for so long, they can't even be found right away. They may be hiding in a corner or locked in a closet. They won't necessarily want a snuggle immediately.

So here's the secret. If the kid is angry or suspicious, it needs to feel that way. Derek's inner kid was so hurt and disappointed, he wouldn't even look at him during the first attempts at contact. Eventually, Derek wrote him a letter of apology for all he'd suffered. A couple weeks later, in a meditation, the kid begrudgingly came and sat in a nearby chair, but still wouldn't talk or touch. Over time, when the boy realized Derek was sincere, he moved closer, and eventually a real friendship unfolded.

You begin wherever you are.

And everyone starts somewhere.

ᴀ SOURCE OF GRATITUDE

As you learn to focus on the child, you'll see it has an innate awareness of appreciation. You know how some kids will say thank you about seven times when you do the smallest thing? You can give them some random rock off the ground, and they're thrilled to pieces.

It may even be intensely thankful to be reconnected to you. Marina had a vivid meditation of opening a locked door and releasing her malnourished, abandoned kid from years of imprisonment. At first, when she hobbled into the light, the girl was so disoriented she could barely speak. She was also spitting mad at Marina for having left her there for so long!

But Marina devotedly returned to her, promising that she could take as long as she needed to heal. One day in meditation, she finally saw the girl crawl happily into her lap for a hug. Marina whispered, *I'll take care of you forever, my sweet princess. You'll never be abandoned again.*

THE INNER CAVALRY

Some people—women in particular—are still waiting for that lover, partner, or friend to save them both emotionally and financially. But often that longing is actually the kid's. The most generous partner in the world could ride up on that legendary white stallion and if your *own* inner caretaking hasn't begun, you *still* won't feel safe. Initially, it's always an inside job with that kid. For everyone.

When it's crying, *Save me, save me.* you learn to reply, *Oh yes, honey,* I will. *I'm finally going to be a wonderful parent for you.* When you, the adult, regain your dignity and no longer move through the world like a starving orphan, others become eager to give to you too. Generosity on the inside brings it on the outside.

You can say, "Let me begin to care for this tender one. Open me, dear Lord, even if I feel resistant at first. Abundance arrives as I care for her more and more."

The kid is usually the one frantically grabbing at the world, yelling, "I want this, I want that, what if I don't get what I need?" It's the one whining (often with good reason), "How come I always feel so cheated?" When you finally start to feed it, the world reshapes itself around you.

JUST SELF-LOVE

Now, the connection to the inner child is not just endless self-indulgence. It's not *All right, you're sad today, so let's blow through every dollar so you feel better.* Instead, you're making an inner sankalpa—that beautiful Sanskrit word meaning intention or vow—to love, support, and stop persecuting it.

Dana wrote, "I'm hard on myself all the time and have massive expectations." When she prayed to treat that child with compassion and kindness, her whole world opened up.

The woman who wrote at the beginning of this chapter about endless clothes and accessories wouldn't need to strip her kid of all shopping privileges. Instead, she might say to her, *Yes. Once a week, we'll buy something.* Or she might include it as she cleans out her closets. The kids *love* to be included, and there are a thousand ways. The more you do, even annoying tasks can become fun.

I have a friend who'd never gotten around to sending thank-you notes a year after her wedding. Every day, she hammered herself for being so irresponsible. Finally, she offered it all to the Divine and saw that her inner child actually was waiting to help.

So she and the kid decided to throw a party. She recruited a couple girlfriends with the promise of non-stop sushi and sake for an evening of "Letters Be Gone."

They ate, drank, blasted music, and made an assembly line with stamps and envelopes. Each time they finished twenty letters, they took a dance break. Her kid had a great time!

This isn't about new laws for enforcement and punishment. As you build healthy boundaries, the child will start to feel supported. Then you can give to it in ways that fit your finances. When it starts to feel nurtured, it will no longer grab.

Besides, one of the keys to eternal youth is your wild, honest, and loving communion with that child. You never lose your own sense of creativity, play, or abandon, no matter the chronological age your body pretends to be.

And the child will blossom happily in the sunlight of your devoted care and attention.

Reading to the Kid

Perhaps because I'm a writer, I especially love the idea of reading to your inner child.

> As my inner kid and I listen to children's books together, I state her feelings back to her. When I notice emotions churning in my belly, I say to her, *You feel furious!* or *You feel so sad right now.* I keep tuning in and stating her feelings as they change, until she relaxes. I release an inner sigh even as I write these sentences. She feels relief that someone has finally seen and heard her; she can relax and let herself be held.

Yes! You can reflect the feelings of your inner kid. Rather than having an argument about why it shouldn't feel what it already does, you just witness and accept its experience. Once the little one is acknowledged without blame, it reliably calms down.

Simply witness the kid. It only wants to be heard and felt.

Besides, if you want to make it feel truly crazy-frustrated, try convincing it to *not* have a deep feeling when it does. Boys, especially—but some girls too—are often told to deny having fear or sadness. But how much healthier we are when the emotions can be acknowledged and released.

A TANGLE OF EMOTIONS

The child can make itself known through your own feelings of sorrow, guilt, shame, or resentment. Sometimes you're deep in a hard emotion and realize, *Oh my god. My kid is crying for help!* Here are a few examples.

THE SECRET WOUND

A few years ago, I went on a weeklong yoga retreat in Cabo San Lucas. It was my idea of heaven: vigorous vinyasa classes all day, a hot tub under the stars by night. But midway, my little one nabbed the wheel.

One day there was an outing to a nearby town. A group bus would go as well as a couple of cars. I asked someone I knew if I might come along in her car.

Well, the *moment* I asked, I sensed she wanted privacy, but she got all weird rather than just saying so directly. (You've probably had this happen. You're just standing there getting doused with terrible energy; suddenly you're six, back on the playground, and no one wants you on their team.)

I quickly backtracked. "No worries, I don't need to come!"

Now, the wiser part of me knew Love was saying, "Hey, this trip isn't needed at all. Just stay at the retreat and write. No need to twist someone's arm."

However, did that take away the suffering? *Oh my god, not at all.* You might even say it all happened to *evoke* the lonely young girl inside who often felt left out.

When everyone left, she cried and cried her little eyes out for hours. It was actually a relief, hitting the mother lode of forgotten pain with total permission to feel. I lay on the bed holding my stomach, sobbing. "It hurts, it hurts . . ." Eventually, the little girl was an exhausted heap on the bed, tired yet happy.

This event may indeed have been Divinely orchestrated to quickly and efficiently cauterize my neglected wound. By dinner, I was even grateful to the curt lady who'd hurt my feelings. If I'd hated her, I would have missed the whole point.

> *Allow me to give compassion and love to that little one.*
> *Let me attend to its deepest needs and feelings.*

UNDER THE TABLE

You mentioned how if someone feels they don't deserve money, they can spend it all compulsively. Could you say more about this? I think there's some shame there, or unworthiness or guilt, because I've sometimes received financial help.

If everything is Divine Source, then up to now, God has sometimes brought you money through the assistance of others. How powerful to be able to say to that ashamed kid, *I finally forgive you. It's okay. This is how you survived. And now God will be showing another way.* It's as if she's hiding underneath a table with the cloth over her, mortified that she's needed any help.

You could imagine that you crawl under there to talk with her. You could let her know she's done the best she could and she's neither bad nor selfish. You can promise to become a protective, loving parent for her, and that a new financial future will unfold.

Perhaps you can also do the coconut ritual from Week Three where you offer all finances back to God. You might also try a Change Me prayer: "May I know I deserve to have abundance. May I know I deserve to have enough."

Because you do.

RAKIA'S REBIRTH

Rakia had been a highly valued tech guru who made bags of money in one company after another. Yet even in the best of times, she'd always lived far beyond her means, incessantly craving the best of the best: Gucci, Prada, Cartier—all of it. She never kept any savings.

Then suddenly she went through a stretch where all her jobs vanished while the overhead of her lavish life remained huge. Eventually, she slid from unbridled spending into anxious unemployment. In a few more months, she hit rock bottom when she couldn't make the payments on her waterfront penthouse. She ended up spending half a year couch surfing with friends.

Rakia had been brought completely to her knees. Until then, she'd always thought she could manifest *anything.* I mean, she used to believe she had such superpowers she'd attracted not just a regular ole Mercedes, but one with self-heating seats for winter.

But with this intense test, Rakia moved into true, unvarnished surrender. She spent nights pleading, "Dear God, I don't know why this is happening and I sure never thought it could! So please, please help me embrace the lessons here. Let me trust that You are the Source of all and can fix this as I let go."

The more she surrendered, the more she realized that she'd clung to all these fancy labels because her mother had never valued her; in fact, she'd barely even looked her way. Rakia saw she needed to cut the virulent cords from her mom. She finally began to care for that dear abandoned girl who'd never felt good enough and always had something to prove. She also stopped blaming herself for falling into this financial mess in the first place.

During those months of getting by on the mercy of friends, Rakia learned to truly give her finances to God for the first time. She honestly had no other choice. Then one day, suddenly, a former employer stopped by, literally plucked her off the green frayed couch in her friend Dave's basement, and offered her a job with the same salary she'd made before. Soon enough, she owned a home again—though a far more modest one so she could build savings. Most important, she had a brand-new relationship to money.

She now knows to her core that the money is God's. She knows what it means to lose it all, and regain it, seemingly from nowhere. She finally respects and honors money as largesse from the Divine.

LET IT RIP!

One of the biggest myths is that spiritual people should never have "bad" emotions. When anger, sadness, jealousy, pain—all of it—are repressed, they often unconsciously spray all over the place instead. The road of this inner communion allows for *all* feelings to be welcomed. There are simple ways to release them without inflicting them on others.

Once they're given permission, emotions are like a thunderstorm or any other force in nature. No reason to think it always has to be tranquil. In fact, the more feelings are allowed, the more they can just pass through like the weather. Yet certain ones—anger, especially—can take special care.

If you have a fiery nature, getting anger out physically may make all the difference. Exertion can go right to the problem in a way that just talking won't. For some people, a vigorous sport like hiking, swimming, or biking is helpful.

But if the anger is huge, some people really need to "destroy" something. My theory is that if you're absolutely furious, it's so much better to break or implode something harmless than send all that firepower against *yourself*.

Personally, I'm a big fan of breaking dishes, the cheapest therapy on the planet. If you're ever wildly mad, go to Goodwill and get a stack of old, cracked plates or cups. Then find a private place and smash the *heck* out of them. Scream if you need to. (Some people even like to scrawl names on what they're breaking.) Better the dishes than your own tender psyche. The anger wants and deserves to come out.

Elsa felt unbearable rage after her divorce. She took it out on herself by eating barrels of popcorn, though it made her so sick she could hardly walk. When I suggested she try this dish therapy, she said, "Oh I need *way*, way more than that!" I suggested she pray for her own route.

She called me the next day, giddy with joy. Her inner kid was so palpable, even on the phone. Elsa had bought about 20 stuffed animals at a thrift store. Then she'd hidden in her garage (so the neighbors wouldn't think she was totally stark raving bonkers) and ripped them to shreds with scissors and knives. Stuffing flew everywhere like a blizzard.

Eventually, she collapsed on the floor, helplessly laughing and surrounded by decapitated teddy bears. She said she'd never had such fun in her life; she'd grown up in a proper British home where she'd never, ever been allowed to get mad.

If you're reading this with horror, I would just ask, Where do you think *all* that violent energy went *before* Elsa did this? Straight into her own poor body and psyche. (And if tearing apart stuffed animals doesn't work for you, you might try mercilessly beating a tightly rolled mattress pad with a baseball bat, another inspired route.)

Everyone's different. For some, anger is easy, and sadness is the stopper in the bottle. Some even use anger to not feel the sorrow underneath.

When my mom died, I couldn't cry for months, though every unshed tear felt like a geyser inside me, ready to blow. Finally, I realized I could turn to sad movies for help, especially animated ones. *Mulan, Up,* and *Ratatouille* all sent me on crying sprees, though I could probably list 20 others as well. Tears are what happen when the ice in the heart melts.

The writer and movie critic Kevin Lincoln wrote a story in *The New York Times* about regaining his ability to cry by going to movies. As a "typical American male," he'd had the ability forced out of him (though I've met people of all genders who have had this happen too).

He wrote how he learned to stop crying, the way so many boys do, as a rite of passage to becoming a man. Eventually in the safe dark zone of movies, he learned "to sit with a moment and be empathetic and vulnerable, to react without an agenda," and to get comfortable with his own tears. It brought back his ability to access and understand his own feelings for the first time since he was a kid.

While some people gain this access through therapy, I love how Kevin turned something as simple as moviegoing into a spiritual communion with that once-neglected child.

For the remaining weeks, get to know your inner kid. Bring it out of hiding, listen to it, include it. Be patient, take it slow, be consistent. Notice what age the kid is. For some people, it will be very young; for others, a teen. (It may also change ages on different days or morph in the course of a single meditation.) And if your own kid is filled with rage, prepare for age-appropriate behavior—tantrums, snubs, hurtful remarks, manipulation. It's all okay. Let it get those feelings out.

If you're not sure how to handle the behavior, aren't seeing results, or are frustrated because a strategy works one day and not the next, don't despair. Just as a parent who's having trouble speed-dials friends for advice, you offer it to Love. If you persevere, you will be rewarded. Through the process of reconnection, a deeper creativity, joy, and contentment will come. In loving that kid, you recover your own sense of wonder.

> I offer this to you, oh Beloved. Allow the wall to fall that separates me from my own vulnerable child. Show the route that reunites us with patience and faith. I long to take care of myself like never before!

WEEK SIX

The Crown Jewels

Detachment is not that you should own nothing,
but that nothing should own you.

— Ali ibn Abi Talib

During my twenties, I used to go to Michael, a terrific intuitive in Berkeley who said one thing like a broken record: "Honey, there's always gonna be *somethin'*." The idea that one day you'll land in a secret spot where no problem ever comes (if you could just keep your mind fanatically clean enough) was complete lunacy. "This too shall pass," he'd say, "but don't forget, it shall pass and bring the same damn thing a second time—or a close proxy—if you don't embrace it the first."

That's why in Week Six, we're going to go deeper into the nature of offering. It's based in radical acceptance, saying yes to Reality in any given moment, so that what's *needed* can come next. It blasts open the door to being abundance.

This week, I'll take you through the key stages of offering I've often witnessed so you can watch them in your own process. But first, we'll need to dive into three concepts.

ᴄHREE LITTLE JEWELS

For a while, a meme was going around the Internet that said, "Relax, everything really *is* out of control!" And yes, from the level of ego, this is entirely true. We all know change is a reliable constant. So if the ego leads, every time something shifts, especially if it seems "negative," it may well throw a hissy fit: *No, I* won't *let go. I refuse!* Or it will spiral into hopelessness or despair. (Yes, the kid is usually the one having these reactions.)

So how do you get past that? Besides comforting and soothing the little one, the answer lies within three beautiful terms: aparigraha, vairagya, and ishvara pranidhana. In the ancient Indian texts the Bhagavad

Gita and Patanjali's *Yoga Sutras*, these are the crown jewels of Existence. Gaining them is a prize far beyond winning an Olympic gold medal, nabbing an Oscar, or being knighted by the queen. When these jewels begin to grace your soul, your feet are firmly on the road to freedom.

Sometimes people say, "Oh, I'm working *sooo* damn hard to surrender. All I do is beat myself up about not being able to let go." The ego will want to make this all an arduous job, but that's just more doership and distraction. As you offer your burdens to Love, you *invite* in these Divine qualities. Eventually, they will come.

They're actually available to anyone, with practice. You can say, "I can't do it, God. I can't! Take over and help me let go." But self-acceptance (and even a rollicking sense of humor) is critical along the way. Your *humanity* is learning to align with the Flow. You keep offering kindness to the kid, saying, *It's okay. Don't worry. All will unfold.*

You might wonder at this point, What *is* that humanity? Well, it's your unique individuality, the small self, the personal expression of you as *you*. The trick of this work is to allow the authentic humanity to remain in all its vibrant glory while at the same time bowing to that inner Divine. In the toggle shift between the Great Self and the small, as time goes on, with prayers and offering, you become fluent at moving between the two.

Once you're on Earth for enough lifetimes, as an old soul you begin to long ever more deeply for these gemstones. They *are* the peace of God. And then, that longing *itself* actually brings the chance to acquire them. You get custom-made, just-for-you opportunities to develop non-grasping, detachment, and surrender.

Remember Prarabdha Karma? Every person has their own personalized study plan in this Earth school. For many old souls, gaining these jewels *is* the core curriculum. If you were learning a foreign language, progressively harder lessons would come as you advanced in skill until you could say anything you needed. Similarly, the Divine has a lesson plan for you to learn to hold these spiritual qualities with ever-increasing fluency.

A simple example: Freya collects antique glassware. One day at a garage sale, she found a highly valuable vase for just 99 cents. Excited beyond measure, she bought it . . . then accidentally dropped it on the way back to her car. If her ego were in the lead, she might have said, *What a klutz! I'm completely destroyed and devastated. Let me blame myself for hours.* But seen through a spiritual lens, she actually got the perfect chance to invite in those jewels, far more valuable than even the shattered antique.

Authors Stephen and Ondrea Levine tell a story about this in *Who Dies?*

They describe a Thai meditation master who was asked how we can find security in a world of impermanence. How can we relax and be happy when nothing stays the same?

> "He answered by holding up a drinking glass and saying, 'You see this goblet? For me, this glass is already broken. I enjoy it. I drink out of it. It holds my water admirably, sometimes even reflecting the sun in beautiful patterns. . . . But when I put this glass on a shelf and the wind knocks it over . . . I say, 'Of course.' When I understand that this glass is already broken, every moment with it is precious. Every moment is just as it is.'"

And that's true offering.

ᏟHE THREE STAGES

Distinct levels of offering can occur in anyone. Once you know them, it's much easier to not get deluded or trapped.

STAGE ONE

Here's the starting line. In this stage, the ego is fully in the driver's seat, saying, *I want what I want. If I don't get it, I'll most definitely feel angry or hopeless, maybe forever.* Resentment, despair, and frustration are familiar emotions. Attempts to control and manipulate reality crop up all day long.

Now, please don't misunderstand me, there's nothing wrong with this. Feelings are fine, and this process sure isn't about blocking them. But this stage is simply a natural expression of the ego steadfastly fighting reality.

And here's what's funny. You could be a rock star with 10 million Instagram fans and still be smack at Stage One. You could even be a "yoga star" with groupies everywhere, and, yep, stuck like glue in Stage One. Because the whole world might be worshipping at your feet while in a way, you're still a slave . . . to your own desires.

STAGE TWO

Here the awareness of offering becomes intellectual. You learn about surrender and inviting the Divine to lead. Often, this stage unfolds from the sheer exhaustion of not getting your desires. You start trying to "turn things over."

However, the *small self* still firmly rules the roost. This stage is the trickiest because you can convince yourself that you've surrendered, when in fact the ego is simply using offering as a strategy to try to get what it wants. For example, *I'll offer my money to the Divine so I can become rich.* You know you've moved to the next stage when you're no longer attached to outcome.

I'll give you an example. I was talking to a friend recently who's quite familiar with these concepts. She complained, "You know, I've got so many decisions to make right now, I feel like my head's gonna explode. Everything's coming at once."

"I know *exactly* what that feels like," I agreed, "but you also know offering! What if you made a list and one by one gave each burden back to God?"

She rolled her eyes and waved her hand at me. "Oh, yeah, yeah," she said, "I know all about offering."

"No," I persisted, perhaps annoyingly. "You know the *idea* of it, but you're still thinking *you* are the one who carries it all."

She went silent for a moment. And then, finally, she got it.

Later she told me she wrote everything down and prayed: "Dear God, help me prioritize. Let me know what matters first, then second, and what doesn't even matter at all. Then please act through me and do it all. I can't possibly handle all of this!"

As soon as she did that, she immediately felt spacious and relieved. And then voila! She moved to Stage Three.

STAGE THREE

In this stage, the *me* no longer carries the cumbersome center of identity. Everything that needs to happen starts to happen without you consciously "doing." *The Universe acts through you.* And the outcome is none of your business.

There's no need to judge or compare any of these stages. They're all just seasons of unfolding, and over time, you may flip from one to another. So eventually, you might be ensconced in Three much of the time, yet occasionally get triggered and even pop back into One, clutching and grabbing obsessively. Then you just breathe and say, *Let me return to what I know: everything is* indeed *out of control and God will hold it all. I can safely let go.*

And then you're back in Three.

⒜PARIGRAHA: NONGRASPING

Aparigraha is one of the deepest secrets of Divine Flow. It means "Let everything that wants to go, go. And everything that wants to come, come." The more the hands open to receive, the less they clutch at everything. Whether we're talking about releasing old identities, belongings, or cords to others, it's all the same.

Aparigraha knows that chasing and attaching reliably pushes away the good that wants to come. It's a doorway to abundance. Think of chasing a feather. The air current you create by reaching and reaching for it keeps pushing it farther away. But if you become still, it may land right in your lap.

In my own life, this has often felt like one of the main remedial courses I was born to take, perhaps one I'd skipped or flunked in past lifetimes. (Oh my god, will you send that girl back to Aparigraha U again until she finally gets it right?) God has smacked my hand *hard* every time I've gripped something too tightly. Eventually, I longed to cooperate.

But here's how bad it used to be. In my twenties, I lived for a while in an apartment building in New York that was so flimsy the water pipes froze and exploded one winter. Relying on the most basic common sense, available even to your average toddler, all the other residents had fled weeks earlier. But I was so terrified I might not find another spot that I became the lone holdout—as water drowned the whole building. Clothes, books, furnishings—everything lost because I didn't trust another landing spot awaited. Yes, I was hanging on *that* hard. (No matter where you fall on the grasping scale, I hope that made you feel a little better. God can change anyone!)

For some of us, learning to let go is a hard-won victory, but for others it seemingly comes naturally. Here are two stories of people who instinctively understood how to embody aparigraha.

THE BLESSED FAILURE

Sometimes a bump in the road or a detour is really a blessing, no matter how maddening it seems. Once, during a huge, glorious storm, I ducked into a ceramics shop in Berkeley. As the rain pelted, I ended up in a conversation with the owner.

He told me that years ago he'd had three galleries and was super "successful." He was so busy he worked from six in the morning till eleven at night.

Then, in the big Bay Area earthquake of 1989, one of his shops was destroyed. People commiserated, "Man, what horrible luck. How sad!" But he noticed how with two stores rather than three, he only worked from eight until seven. His life was simpler.

A few years later, massive fires came to the Oakland hills, and his second location burned to ashes. At that point, a friend said, "Dude, I've *never* known a nicer, sweeter guy who's been more cursed. Bad luck follows you like a love-starved puppy."

"But," the owner said, grinning, "who really knows?" Because finally, with only *one* shop, his hours were nine to five, something he'd never even imagined.

Of course, by then, he had less money and needed to sell his large home. But his wife and kids were so thrilled to finally have time with him that no one cared much. They moved into a smaller place and became a real family for the first time.

"So, was it bad luck or good?" he asked me.

I smiled and looked outside.

A faint rainbow hung over the horizon.

ORANGE IS THE NEW BLACK

Isn't it strange to hear "Never give up" when sometimes that's the most important spiritual tool you can use? For an old soul, sometimes nothing can change until *you* do. The Emmy-winning actor Uzo Aduba had to release her most passionate desire: to perform. She broke out of her prison of attachment only to end up incarcerated in a role of a different kind.

Uzo was playing in *Godspell* in New York City and auditioning for television pilots, waiting for her big break. It went like this: Try, try, try, followed by no, no, no. One day, she finished a particularly critical audition, feeling things had gone well yet sensing she still wouldn't be picked since she'd been 20 minutes late. This failure, she reasoned, would be "God's Universe" telling her, "this is *not* for you, so stop trying to take something that's not yours." On the subway home, she "prayed it up" for a clear sign to quit acting and head to law school. She surrendered fully.

Forty-five minutes later, right after walking into her apartment, she got a phone call. The part of Suzanne "Crazy Eyes" Warren in the TV show *Orange Is the New Black* was dropped straight into her lap.

VAIRAGYA: DETACHMENT

Vairagya means even more than detachment. I love that it actually means *without color*, as in "you see clearly, without the tint of emotions and desires." You may have preferences, but you're not at the mercy of them.

Often people will cavalierly say, "Well, it is what it is," but down deep they actually mean *Screw this! I completely* hate *that it is what it is*. But vairagya is when you really feel *I can accept this*.

It's part of radical acceptance. The overlay of resistance falls away.

You think, *It's just how it is* right now. *An hour later, all could be different.*

THE SACRED MEAL

When a particularly intense desire has been cooked in the fires of offering, it transmutes into a preference. And often the process is painful as hell because lifetimes of attachments, delusions, and addictions are being stripped away. You may feel as though you're bathing in turpentine.

But over time, when the offering is sincere, you become free of that bondage. You soften and let go. You feel neutral and spacious.

Vairagya has come.

You know when it's arrived because you no longer feel shackled.

You're no longer a totally crazed addict.

You finally feel whole in your own skin, with *or* without the delivery of that desire.

You might even passionately adore receiving this "whatever," but you're no longer enraged or dispirited without it.

That's often exactly when the preference can finally be received and enjoyed . . . as a *sacred meal.*

Allow me, Divine, to offer You my deepest longings, trusting You to know exactly how to handle them. Lead the way and free me from my chains. And please let me know my own wholeness and freedom most of all.

So here's a story about vairagya. Someone thinks they're going to get their big break, but their desire strangles them like a boa constrictor. Vairagya allows them to get free.

No One Is Your Source (No, Not Even Oprah)

A few years ago, after a vinyasa class, I ran into an author I knew. When I asked how things were going, he wondered, smiling, if I wanted to hear about his "writing tragedy." Of course!

He told me he'd come out with a big yoga book, and a friend offered to get him on *SuperSoul Sunday.* He was beside himself with excitement. Finally, he'd be discovered. He saw the Broadway marquee of his future stardom glimmering around the next bend.

And then . . . the test began. His interview was scheduled, then changed. And changed again. On the final round, it was moved *up* to where he only had 48 hours to prepare.

He was horrified that Amazon would have no time to fill their coffers with his book. He begged for another date to no avail. He'd finally be getting his "big break" without his work even being available.

This threw him into such despair, he was little more than a robot on the show. Laughing, he told me that he might be the only author ever featured by Oprah to have *zero* happen.

But I had a different perspective. Maybe he didn't get the riches he was expecting, but what if he'd gotten something far more valuable? After all, he'd written a book on yoga, which in Sanskrit actually means *yoked to the Divine*. What if God took him on that wild voyage to acquire vairagya? What if it was one of those perfectly handcrafted-for-his-own-freedom experiences? What if it made him a true yogi and not just a chaser of outcomes? What if he could finally let go?

Feel, Then Offer
Detachment is sometimes mistaken for turning off feelings or going numb. It's certainly not "spiritual bypassing," which means ignoring the most vulnerable parts of our human selves to sound evolved. No, not at all. It just means you feel, then offer.

The other day, my friend Loreen told me how frustrated she was as a stepmother to three kids. For help, she'd been listening to a certain recording about detachment. It said, "Just turn off all bad feelings and refuse to indulge them. Lock them in a vault."

"So how's that working for you?" I laughed.

She winced. "Terribly. I'm furious. So many ridiculous things that have gone down. I've put everybody's needs ahead of my own for years, yet continue to be scapegoated anyway. How could I just shove this away? Can't I *have* feelings?"

I wholeheartedly agreed, suggesting she write everything down and burn it. Then do everything possible to really *feel* those emotions. (We discussed many ways in Week Four.) A coconut could also be broken as an offering. As Loreen did this, she began to see how she needed to set much stronger boundaries with everyone in the family.

Vairagya comes through owning that precious vulnerability of our feelings, then offering it all. If you just hide your emotions in some psychic footlocker, they're guaranteed to detonate later, causing much suffering and misunderstanding.

Feelings can indeed be felt and then offered. This brings detachment . . . and the right action at the right time.

Ishvara Pranidhana: surrender

Surrender is at the core of being Abundance. You move into a joyous flow of giving and receiving. You let yourself be used by the Divine.

As true offering arises, it becomes easy to let go, because you start to trust that *more* will always come in. You make the shift from *mine . . . mine . . . mine* to *God's . . . God's . . . God's.* Such a difference!

For the last 11 years, I gave everything to an expensive manifesting program and chased every longing. I became so exhausted that I could barely see straight. But here's what's funny. All that time, I'd been visualizing a work-at-home job. Nothing ever happened. But after just a month of surrendering and doing the Change Me Prayer, my current company simply handed me that job. Same pay, same benefits, and no two-hour commute. Thank you for explaining offering in such a practical way.

It's easy to fall into blaming yourself for "failure at manifesting." But that's all based in Stage One thinking, at the level of ego. Instead, learning to surrender and open to Source will often solve the problem.

Over time, reciting the Full Abundance Change Me Prayer brings a Divine cushion that holds and supports you. You're no longer in freefall. Many of your fears may well evaporate. You start to trust you'll be okay with or without your desire; you tap into the peace that comes when demands end. You sense that every true need will *indeed* be met, one way or another.

Once you make room for this holy plan, you no longer insist, "My way at all cost!" You start to say, "God, show me how to live this. Let me at least pretend for now that You are truly my Provider." As you open this way, prosperity can come from unlimited, unexpected sources. Love is far more creative than the rigid, constrained, yet exhausted ego.

I'm scared if I let go and surrender to the Divine, I won't get what I really want.

One of the biggest misconceptions is that the Divine is *separate* from us. But when you understand that you're actually surrendering to your own inner Great Self, your own wisdom and clarity, it's so different. (However, as you know from Week Five, often this involves becoming the committed parent of that terrified kid.)

And here's the truth: Love always runs the show whether we surrender or not. A brand-new world shimmers open when you choose to cooperate.

LET'S MAKE A DEAL

I get that we're learning from every experience, but the ones that are challenging are hella challenging! So why can't the Divine just send a lesson plan or something? Why must this always feel like an episode of *Let's Make a Deal*, where you guess what's behind the door?

Anyone else remember that game show? I watched it every day after junior high school. If you picked the correct door, you might win a set of living room furniture, a freezer full of ice cream sandwiches, or a ski boat. But if you're an old soul, the prize behind each door is aparigraha, vairagya, or ishvara pranidhana.

And that's the lesson plan too. If we instantly got every desire here on Earth, there'd be no incentive to develop these sacred qualities.

Very often people find my work because the "other way" of chasing and grasping has crashed and burned like a meteor. But that painful destruction is a moment of tremendous grace as well. Because when the ego finally sees the utter madness of trying to control and lead, you come to a sacred crossroads in your own evolution.

Someone once said to me, "The angels all applaud when this letting go occurs." You're finally ready to let something greater than the ego take over. True intimacy with the Divine can begin.

This is the road to freedom, but not because all longings vanish. Instead, desires melt into preferences and no longer *own* you.

Of course, when things get challenging, it's natural to have preferences. The other night, I deeply preferred that my cat not throw up that hairball in bed with me. I equally preferred not to lose five hours of writing as I did last week when my Mac crashed out of nowhere.

But here's how it goes: Your interest in true offering takes precedence over all else because the soul is *hell-bent* on freedom. Hell-bent.

This exquisite way is straight out of the ancient scriptures. And isn't it lovely to know that this route can be done in modern-day life and not just 10 centuries ago in India or Persia? God is just as numinous and available as ever!

So what if you look at your life right now without any judgment and ask, *Which quality am I learning? Which crown jewel?* Whatever comes to mind first is your curriculum.

For example, let's say you recently lost a job that you were very attached to. It could be a chance for ishvara pranidhana, or surrender into what is. You're not having to accept it forever, only for this exact moment. By opening to Divine Source, something superior can come next.

By the way, be careful not to confuse these three crown jewels with passivity. They actually bring the ability to act with increased clarity and courage because you're no longer attached to outcome.

ᗡHE EXALTED BARISTA

I have a theory that many of the most evolved beings on the planet aren't in the limelight whatsoever. They're just "regular" folks living with joy, dignity, and sometimes laserlike precision. Like Carmina.

For a long time, I've gone to a certain café and noticed this barista in her twenties. In the early morning hurricane of orders, she's total equanimity and cool. One day,

I watched a guy scream at her when she gave him soy instead of skim. She responded with total kindness and serenity. Yesterday someone else went at her, and once again, pure love. She's a dancing warrior princess behind the counter, juggling cups, cinnamon, and foam.

"Carmina, how the heck do you do this?" I asked. "It's brutal being a barista. A friend of mine quit after two days."

She laughed. "*Dios mio*, you're so right, but four years ago I figured it out. You can control almost nothing but your reaction. So I decided to become a master of that. Then each day I can practice. The biggest *locos* give you the best workout!"

> *Allow me, Divine, to move with the Flow and respond with calmness and peace. I am Yours. You are mine. We are One. All is well.*

OFFERING EQUALS SURRENDERING

As we discussed, surrender often gets confused with passivity, or even hopelessness. But it's simply the release of attachment: whether to the five hundred dollars for a car payment, the partner you can't live without, or the baby you feel you must have.

You simply cannot fully offer without surrender. You give the longing to Love.

In a sense, you say:

> *Help me trust that all deepest needs will be met. Let me enter this path of freedom. Even my deepest attachments, I give to You. Let me trust You have a plan and the right actions will come. You are my Source for all.*

Sometimes an offering is fulfilled instantly. Sometimes, later or not at all. You start to trust the process.

You say to Love, "Take me over and unclench my hands. May all be handled perfectly."

Through offering, even the most mundane problem can become a sacrament.

⊂THE CUSTODY BATTLE

Sheila had long been in a terrible legal battle over her son, a horror movie with constant new sequels (*The Lying, Cheating Ex Returns: Parts X, XI, XII* . . .). She'd been ardently visualizing full custody forever. Yet, for all these efforts, everything remained in frozen acrimony. She'd spent hundreds of thousands of dollars on attorneys.

Finally, despite feeling apprehensive about the outcome, she began to offer. After all, what could be harder than to surrender your own flesh and blood? But for her own sanity, she began to say, "Yes, he's my son, but in truth, he's God's. I offer all to You for a Divine plan. I can't keep telling You how to do it." She was finally able to pray, "May this happen for the highest good for all."

That concept in particular was huge, since she was so furious she sure didn't want anything good for her ex. She *wanted* him to suffer. Nonetheless, she said, "I can't take it anymore. May this finally happen for the Highest. This child is God's." While in the beginning this prayer felt mechanical, over time she truly felt it.

Soon after, the ex abruptly left the picture, with little fanfare. He moved back to his native Germany, saying, "You know what? *You* really want to be a parent, and I actually never did. I just wanted to win." She got full custody—not from clobbering the Universe with her desires, but from sincerely *letting go.*

Just letting go.

OLD SOUL TEEN

One day, in a shop on Chestnut Street in San Francisco, I overheard a mom on her phone: "Yeah, we all head back to L.A. tomorrow. But tonight, at the beach, we'll do one more big ceremony and make sure the Universe knows *we mean business!* We'll uplevel and attract that down payment for the chalet by Tuesday, don't you worry. We can rock this! And if we all vibrate at the exact right frequency according to that protocol, we *will* make it happen. We are powerful. I can't wait!"

I watched as her uber-adorable teenage daughter in a backward baseball cap and chopped-off hair gave a loud, exasperated sigh, as if she'd been hearing this very conversation since she was a zygote.

"Um, Mom," she said, rolling her eyes and shaking her head dramatically, "what if the Universe just has a different freakin' *plan* than yours?"

I giggled, and the girl gave me a thumbs-up with an impish smile.

And I thought, *Oh my god, now here's what happens when the* kid *is the ancient one in the family.* Some old souls are born innately understanding surrender, but for the rest of us, dedicated prayer and offering over time absolutely brings the same results.

Just keep going.

No, You're Not Crazy, You're Being Tested

Be crumbled so wildflowers will come up where you are.
You have been stony for too many years.
Try something different. Surrender.

— Rumi

Once I got a fortune cookie that read, "Through God's design you will pass the Imperial Examination." I mean, what kinda fortune is that? My dinner companion got "Good luck is on the horizon."

But in this process of learning to let the Divine lead, you really *are* tested. Often. Sometimes in ways that even try your sanity. Not in a punishing way, but as if Love says, "Is this spiritual understanding *real* and not just a nice idea?"

There's a Zen story about a group of students who were sent to construct a bridge. When they finished, the teacher jumped on it hard to see whether it would collapse. Many times, God does the same.

He tests the bridge for its solidity before letting you cross and move on. When I have this happen to me, I know the Divine is making sure I'm not just sounding good. Perhaps I had that disconnect between words and actions in some past lives, but this time around, like Cheryl Lynn sang in the '70s, it's "Got to Be Real."

Now, as you've been moving along with the Abundance steps, you may have seen miracles sprouting everywhere like dandelions in the summer. Perhaps prosperity keeps pouring from unexpected places—all of a sudden somebody gives you an amazing sweater in your favorite color or free tickets to a concert you've always wanted to attend. Truly, that's one way this path can unfold. But since you're inviting Love to steer, a whole other experience may come instead.

For example, you might have temporary losses that test your faith in the Flow. Or, despite feeling more positive and renewed, money might still seem as elusive as ever. Many people naturally get angry, dispirited, or frustrated when they're being tested. If a desire is blocked or a promising road doesn't pan out, they can even feel betrayed. But that's all based on the false premise that every desire is meant to be instantly fulfilled at any given moment. Instead, from a spiritual perspective, tests often come to build aparigraha and vairagya.

If you apply yourself to the steps, you'll begin to have the visceral experience that *it's not your money.* You'll come to know this in your Being, not as some lofty spiritual idea you could say to impress (or alarm) people at a cocktail party.

And once this begins to occur, oh my god, get ready. You open to an expansiveness and freedom from the incessant financial worry that plagues most people (unless, of course, they live in Scandinavia). Because, you see, *that* is the end goal. So if your inner and outer states don't match up yet, fear not. A lot can happen between now and the final part of this process, let alone in the months and years that follow.

ᖯHE DIVINE DECOY

One of my favorite concepts is the Divine decoy because I used to be led astray by it so often myself. This often arrives to burn away attachments and can happen with anything—a relationship, a house, a vacation. Often people get furious: "Okay, God, You made it *seem* like that was the perfect potential job and then after I dressed up and schlepped to seven interviews halfway across the state, they finally said no. Why did you trick me? Seriously, You say You're a God of Love?"

But it was all to learn to let go.

So, if one of these decoys comes your way, don't think the story is over. You just go back to Divine Order and say the perfect "whatever" is already picked and you'll be guided to it in the right time and way. In the world of Divine Source, you *cannot* miss what's Yours.

The decoy's like weight training at a local aparigraha gym. You're sent something alluring to see if you get all clingy about it. Every time you don't attach or obsess, your detachment muscles get stronger.

Of course, at first when a disappointment comes for the ego, you might think, *Forget this God stuff. It doesn't work.* But over time, as the aparigraha muscle grows, you stop falling for the decoy. You naturally learn how to maintain open-handed receiving. You know if one route falls through, another will come. You want what God wants.

Now let's go to some other tools that are invaluable during tests. As you practice them, you'll begin to feel your inner power develop and your faith in the Flow deepen.

Pray for Courage

During the course, many people asked how to summon courage, perhaps to leave a bad relationship that had financial ramifications or to quit a job where they felt unvalued or even abused. Since this process is about letting Love transform you, courage can come through prayer and grace. Divine confidence blooms in a way that's so different from the ego's false bravado. It can have a larger-than-life, preternatural calm. It can even be modest and unassuming, without making a big fuss about itself. Over time, Divine confidence becomes your constant ally and Love grows it within you like a wild, fragrant garden.

You become filled with the strength, inspiration, and conviction *to do what must be done.* You can use this (as

I do) for something as small as making a difficult phone call or as large as leaving a career.

You pray:

> *Take me over and do this through me. If You wish it done, speak through me, act through me. I am Yours alone.*

As you do this, you're petitioning Love itself to take the wheel.

This approach is so different from spanking yourself to get motivated. I have to admit when I hear people snap, "Just put on your big girl (or boy) pants and *do it!*" I can't help but roll my eyes. As you can see, there's a whole other, less punitive way.

> I have a part-time job, with full-time headaches, yet I'm scared that the money won't come from elsewhere. On top of that, a misguided sense of loyalty makes me stay. But in truth, I want to move forward with my own new business and let it flourish. I long to be able to just say, "Adios!" Can you help me with this?

The first step is to offer your current job to the Divine: "If I have anything left to learn here, please make that clear. But if I'm only clinging from fear, then grant me the courage to go and show the timing and the way."

I've done similar prayers with people who sometimes could quit the next day. But if it's not time yet, you'll be stopped, because offering isn't about forcing a decision.

You simply give God the room to be included: "Show me the right actions. If I need to be patient for now, then please keep me from leaving. But if it's long overdue, make me ready!"

As you strengthen your grounding in Divine Source, you remember that Love can use *anything* to sustain you. Your current job is not your Source, only God. The right next means of income is already selected, and you *will* be guided.

Personally, I've been in situations where I felt as if God picked me up by the scruff of my neck and just carried me out. A couple of those times, I knew if I hadn't been forcibly removed in that Divine way, I might have clung so stubbornly, I could have died there. (Remember my frozen pipes?)

Because if you're stubborn yourself, your ego may keep you anchored somewhere long, long past its expiration date. You may think, *I hate it, but it's all I've got.* But when you begin to say, "You alone are my Source for all," you'll know that money can come from anywhere.

By the way, don't fear if you get the answer "Not yet." Perhaps more time is needed for everything to line up. Meanwhile, you can pray for patience. And while you're at it, prayers for acceptance, confidence, and ease work too.

Though I'm not conventionally religious, parts of the Bible speak to me deeply. And when it says, "do not lean on your own understanding" (Proverbs 3:5), that, indeed, is the crux of offering. You lean on Love like a sturdy redwood.

> Over the years I've become filled with fear and procrastination. But during this Abundance process, I've prayed to face them both. I had mercury fillings professionally removed from my mouth after saying, "I offer you, Divine, my 1970s dentistry." I cleaned my home: "Okay, God, here are a few hundred books I no longer need. Please share with others as You wish." I even asked my husband to make a new website for my artwork. He did a great job without one argument. That alone was a miracle. What a blessing to feel courageous again!

Part of the goal is to return you to your own inner knowing, your innate Divine courage and curiosity. You give your intuition full rein to take over. You break free from the stultifying myth that your ego has manifested every dang problem and that you must perfect yourself in order to wrangle free. (Do you feel the utter exhaustion of all that? Oh my god, I sure did.)

Instead, you become an ally to the inner kid who learned all that toxic perfectionism. You soothe the fevered mind that fears if it makes a mistake, bad will come. Little by little, Love takes over.

After a long winter, Divine courage starts to bloom.

Courage Meditation

Focus on your breath for a moment, breathing in calming energy and breathing out any worry or fear.

Imagine you're somewhere in nature that feels wonderful. You might be at the ocean or in a forest, or somewhere else that feels healing to you, in weather you love. If you love the sun, let it come. I love wind, so I imagine a windy day.

Then you can pray to this force of Love that encompasses every-thing, including you. You can say, "I am ready. Fill me with Divine courage. Fill me with Divine confidence. Give me the ability to act when it's time to act, and patience when it's time to wait. Fill me with faith, fill me with trust. Let these Divine qualities come." You can even open your hands to the sky and say, "I am ready. Fill me with your Divine confidence. May I learn to honor what I truly need instead of everyone else's opinion. May I listen inside to your Divine voice."

Feel, for a moment, energy pouring into you. It's always been your birthright. You can pray for it to be available whenever you need.

"Fill me with your courage and confidence. Free me from the prison of my small self and let the right actions arise at the right time."

You may hear a few words on the inside as you do this.

And then, as you're ready, you can slowly come back. Take a moment to write down anything that happened.

Follow Your Intuition

Learning to follow the thread of inner guidance is a big part of our process. You can apply it to anything, big or small, as you'll see in this story.

Many years ago, I was in a spiritual group that had a truckload of dictates about what was "dharmic" and "proper," from music to clothing to food. Many of us twisted ourselves into pretzels each day trying to comply. But eventually, I saw that few knew how to listen inside to what their own souls actually needed. Perhaps it's why I now believe so passionately that true direction comes from the Divine intuition ablaze in our *own hearts*.

One of the group's zillion rules was to *never* wear black. Maybe an occasional dark skirt or pair of pants was okay, but nothing else. We were ominously warned, "Black darkens the heart."

Uber-responsible Capricorn that I was, I promptly ditched all my beloved black clothes (which, as a former New Yorker, was at least half my wardrobe). I was heartbroken.

Then, about a year later, I saw a group of Zen priests robed in black on the New York subway. I suddenly woke from my dutiful sleepwalk: *Oh my god, how ridiculous, I love black! It feels protective and spiritual to me. Do all those priests have dark hearts too?* I started giggling at the craziness of it all.

> *Oh my Lord, wake me from life as a spiritual sheep.*
> *May I hear You through my own instincts and common sense.*

When I bought a new round of beloved funky black T-shirts and jackets, I almost sang with relief. This was *me*, exactly as God had designed. You *know* when your own soul is happy. You don't need anyone else to corroborate it.

Each person's road to the inner Lord is extraordinary and personal. How liberating to listen inside and sense moment to moment what's needed. There's a wild and impetuous uniqueness to you that can be honored. What's poison for one person might be the best of all medicines for another.

In fact, your inner kid will often guide you straight to what brings joy.

Trust yourself.

DOWNRIGHT BAD ADVICE

Most Mondays, I head to an early morning yoga class in Berkeley. At that hour, there's usually plentiful free parking, but one time, all the meters were filled. Tons of yellow zone remained, but as I went to park there, something inside kept nagging: *What if yellow becomes illegal at 8 instead of 9 like the meters?*

I prayed for a sign.

At that moment, a geeky-looking bespectacled guy walked by, so I asked, "Hey there, is yellow okay until nine?"

He snapped back, "Of *course* it is! Don't the meters start then? Why on earth would yellow start first?"

So I listened. And came back to a $59 ticket.

Now, it might have been easy to go into Divine decoy-dom: "Why the heck did You mislead me, God? I asked for help and *this* bozo, in all of Berkeley, is who You send?"

But instead, it was perfect. My own *body* had been warning, *Watch out.*

This guy's answer represented every time I'd deferred to the confident but often clueless responses of others. I was reminded that your instincts will always show you. If something feels wrong, it usually *is.*

As you know by now, it's God's moolah, so there's no gain or loss as long as you offer and don't stay stuck. I dropped the whole matter. The next week, a check arrived for books I'd sold two years earlier—for $60.

No More Than Can Be Handled

Sometimes what lies ahead is so daunting, the mind can neither prepare for nor comprehend it. But often the mind is the confuser, and not the best guide.

Instead, as you offer, breath by breath and moment by moment, the body *itself* shows the next right action. The inner tug, or spanda, is always there, prompted by the instincts; you feel pulled to start or stop, go here or there. But to follow it, you must stay in the present and not get too far ahead of the Flow. If you don't race ahead, you start to trust that nothing more will come than can be handled in each moment.

And if needed, Grace will do the rest in a secret and miraculous way.

WATCH FOR SIGNS

Part of the playful way the Divine interacts with us is through signs and omens. It can be a lot of fun to begin to start paying attention. Keep your eye out for clues that you're on the right path. If you've wandered off course, you'll often get shown how to find your way back.

LANDBIRDS AND TWIGS

In *The Game of Life and How to Play It*, Florence Scovel Shinn writes about how before Columbus reached America, he saw landbirds and twigs, indicating that turf was near. She remarks that it's the same when a problem is cast to the Divine. An initial sign comes to make clear that your prayer has been heard, but it's easy to mistake that for its fulfillment.

Florence uses the example of a woman who needed a set of dishes and offered over the longing. Soon after, a friend gave her an old, cracked plate. The woman complained that this was hardly what she'd requested.

But to Florence, this was all perfect. The broken dish was a portent of this woman's coming good.

THE BREAD CRUMB TRAIL

Yasmeena worked in the design department of a corporation, but dreamt every day of returning to her roots as an artist. Since she had minimal savings, she didn't want to impulsively quit, only to regret the decision later. She offered it all and prayed for a sign.

She was at the farmers market one day when someone said, "I heard you paint portraits. Do you have any time?" Because only a few friends knew about her talent,

Yasmeena was floored. This was her nudge: "Let your painting business unfold."

From only that one inquiry, Yasmeena felt prompted to make a website and post her work on Instagram. The woman from the market eventually became her de facto fairy godmother and referred many others. Eventually, Yasmeena was able to cut her corporate job to part-time. She felt as if the Divine was saying, "Just relax and be where you are for now, and once you build up more of your own work, you'll sense when to fully leave." A year later, she did.

The Divine will show the specifics, but only when you stop grasping onto your current job as your Source.

> *This is now Yours. Make it clear. If I'm meant to go, give me the courage and show me the way.*

SECRET WEAPON

Yushiko was a crackerjack trial attorney renowned for being able to win even the toughest cases. But one had dragged on forever, and no matter what she did, she had no luck.

Yushiko felt utterly defeated.

One night, at the end of her rope, she began to pray her buns off. And let me tell you, this was not a prayin' kind of gal—more like a self-made Wonder Woman. But she had two days until her next court date, so nothing to lose.

Suddenly, for no immediately obvious reason, Yushiko felt drawn to yank one of many huge law tomes off her shelf. Then she closed her eyes, opened the book, and let her finger land.

When she looked at where she pointed, she started crying. She'd gone *straight* to the one argument that had eluded her for four years.

And yes, Yushiko won the case. Big-time.

Praying, casting the burden, and offering are like having access to true superpowers. Why on earth wouldn't you use them?

INVITE HELP

Sometimes you may need to pray for help, though it can be easy to forget.

One day, I was on I-880 heading past Oakland when I ended up behind a stalled car. Even with my arm out, no one would let me change lanes. I tried not to panic as the roar of traffic whizzed by.

Eventually, I remembered to ask, "Please, *please*, send the one who will free me."

A moment later, a trucker slowed down, flashed his lights, and beckoned.

I only had to ask! But don't feel bad if you forget. It took me a whole 10 minutes to remember.

> *Allow me, Divine, to always accept the right assistance. I welcome Your help in every way and delight in receiving it.*

HONOR THE COSMIC CLOCK

People often feel tested when they're not getting the timing the ego wants.

For 30 years, I did counseling sessions with callers from all over the world. Eventually, I began to feel quite confined and yearned to write and teach as I do now.

However, here's the funny thing: the Universe didn't seem to care my small self was bristling for a change. No matter what I tried, I was stuck like glue for five more years in that occupation. I announced classes that never filled and programs that were uniformly ignored by my clients. It just wasn't time yet. Those final years felt like crawling on hot sand while scorpions nibbled my toes.

When I was ultimately "allowed" to stop, I saw I'd been systematically prepared for a major turning point. But the longing to quit arose *years* before I was fully ready.

By the time that agonizing process of surrender was over, my work finally belonged to God. I could live what I taught. I mean, how can you teach letting go when you can't do it yourself?

Once it was time, She flung open the gates with abandon. *Outrageous Openness* started to sell briskly and people began to want the courses they'd blithely dismissed earlier. The light had turned from red to green. It was go time!

So, say you're wishing to move from a particular job to your own gig. Offer it to Love: "You know the timing. You know the way." Now, perhaps the shift will organically come faster than you'd imagined. However, you might be held in check for a while, just as I was. You might be chomping at the bit while invisible yet critical preparation is underway.

If you only look at timing from an ego-based Law of Attraction mind-set, you might think, *I keep visualizing it . . . I keep hammering at the Universe. I keep saying what I want—but the damn doors just won't open. I must need more coaching.*

But a Divinely-timed spiritual birth is so different. You offer the whole situation: "You know my talents. You know my abilities. I long to be of service. If You want this change to come, please show me the first steps."

This isn't wishful thinking, passivity, or hoping for the best. It's actually quite concrete. You cast the burden and ask to be shown the way. If no prompts come, either externally or through the inner spanda, then you might be in that Divine holding tank, being prepared. But fear not, when it's time to act, you will! Sometimes you're even resting up for the new time, because once it comes, you'll be going full-out.

Especially those last couple years of doing sessions, I felt *profoundly, utterly, crushingly done*—yet the Universe knew to not open the gate. When it was time, the big changes happened almost overnight.

And even if the shift takes a while, it doesn't necessarily mean you're doing *anything* wrong.

Just keep offering.

Cooking Pie

In this way of Being, decisions make *themselves* when the time is right.

When in doubt, sometimes the best thing you can do is be exactly where you are, even if you're completely confused.

Sometimes you're being protected from what you don't yet need. *The situation is cooking.*

If you're hitting obstacle after obstacle, simply let it all cook more. What seems like a huge hassle now could be easy as pie later . . . and anyway, do you really want to eat some gooey mess?

Later, it will be delicious.

Because. It. Will. Be. *Ready.*

Being the Abundant Road

You don't need to know the Way.
The Way knows the Way.

— Anonymous

Just like plants in a garden, everyone opens at a different pace. You may notice three or six months from now, *Wow! I'm no longer worrying about money every minute. Somehow, I'm trusting that what needs to come will come. I'm not scared to be generous. I'm not harassing myself any longer for prior mistakes.*

As you continue to do the five steps for this final week and then for however long you need—you might continue daily or just resume as prompted—old patterns will continue to melt. It's like popping ice cubes out of one of those old-fashioned plastic trays. When you first pull the tray from the freezer, you *really* have to work it, twisting right and left, up and down. You might get one lone cube to pop out, but as you continue to twist and the ice melts slightly, many cubes jump free at once.

These steps are similar. With time and practice, patterns begin to release more easily. This isn't because you're trying *harder*, but because you're finally allowing the Divine to take the heck over. It becomes natural to welcome the Flow. You may see finances shift dramatically and opportunities arise from the most surprising places. The road isn't always direct, smooth, or without obstacles, but the more you offer, the more you stay anchored in Source.

Offering is truly the foundation. It's the opposite of everything we're taught, and it takes practice. And for it to be real, there simply *has* to be detachment from outcome.

SO LITTLE TIME, SO MUCH RECEIVING!

Perhaps for the first time in your life, you may see your finances change dramatically, or you may simply notice that your ability to receive is opening like mad. I love the specificity of this woman's list because in the Divine's world, nothing is trivial. Anything can be a harbinger of your unfolding good.

So many fabulous things have come as a result of offering, hearing the course, and saying the abundance prayer daily. They come so fast and frequently, it's both joyous and humorous to list them:

- Found $20 in the pocket of an old coat that was begging me to put it on

- Another $20 from someone who claimed they'd accidentally left it out of my Xmas gift

- Pertinent Messages from audiobooks and commercials that arrived the instant I offered

- Snow days precisely when I needed to catch up on work

- Someone with no idea about a certain medical condition I have handed me a book with every needed remedy

- And most amazingly, no more guilt for dropping an array of psychic vampires from my life

And there are too many more to continue. I'm having a blast offering; I find it better than any entertainment. Answers and solutions pop up constantly, and even no answer feels like one too; it's just "not yet" or "not needed." I can barely remember how I used to stumble along in the dark, so confused, yet not including God.

"MY" BITES THE DUST

It's one thing to understand surrender in an intellectual way, like Stage Two of offering during Week Six. Then, it's just a nice idea. I remember reading countless spiritual books that said you *should* let go. And I'd think, *Really? How?? You can't fake it. When your ego wants something desperately, how do you do this?* One of the most reliable ways is the release of *my*, which immediately lifts you into Stage Three of offering.

So many spiritual writings talk about surrender, but until this work I simply didn't understand how to do it. I just knew that I couldn't keep making life so hard.

At 40, I finally found my purpose informing educators about student trauma. However, although I'd been a teacher myself for 14 years, I couldn't reach decision makers at schools to get booked. You helped me see that "my" workshop actually needed to be the Divine's.

So I gave everything back to Her, and said I longed to serve. Soon after, I found the perfect video about the workshop. I shared it on Facebook, and within two hours, a friend I haven't talked to in 15 years wrote back. She's a principal who was looking for someone to talk about this very topic. For me, trying to twist arms and cajole people had been torture. This felt so easy and right.

Some business coaches advise, "You must get out there and sell yourself. Cold-call a hundred people a day. Don't be lazy!" You hear how you *should* do this or that, and you think, *Can I get back to you on that? Because to be honest, I'd rather jump off a bridge.* To many people, this aggressive approach can feel traumatic and futile. It's just another kind of doership.

Instead, you offer the project to the Divine. You untangle yourself from "my lofty goals and aspirations." You decorate yourself with the crown jewels of aparigraha, vairagya, and ishvara pranidhana. You say, "Okay, God, if You want this to happen, then open the way. Let the connections come. Let everyone who needs me find me."

At the right time, the splendid march of synchronicities begins.

And here's one of the biggest delights and miracles of this route. When you begin to *give* on God's behalf, your own needs get met as well. You serve life, and it serves back. Of course, this doesn't mean you never have challenges, but rather that you're provided for in ever more surprising and beneficent ways. You're on the Divine payroll.

> The concept of "being on God's payroll" has been more comforting to me than I could have ever imagined. What a welcome paradigm shift. I finally understand that you become the *steward* of Divine funds. You distribute Its money when you pay bills or give to others. This is fantastic!

Now, perhaps some of you are thinking, *You know, I'm almost through with this book, and to be honest, I still don't really know if this Divine Source exists. A part of me continues to think this all smacks of wishful thinking and California hocus-pocus.* Well, I'm here to say, I understand that. That's the habitual conditioned part. (And actually, my own East Coast Jewish roots give me a special affection for bemused cynics.) Nonetheless, here's what I still suggest. As an experiment, go *past* the place where the mind wants to keep you stuck.

Go back to offering.

You have absolutely nothing to lose.

Moving with the Flow

Part of being on the road of abundance (or, to be even more precise, becoming the road yourself) is observation. Pay attention. Moving with the Flow from one checkpoint to another. As you know, with your invitation, God can use anything or anyone. Sometimes people do things on your behalf without even knowing why.

Because you have said yes, God takes over.

I'd needed a new iPhone for ages, but hadn't gotten around to getting it. Then one morning while waiting for the ferry to San Francisco, my phone fell, and the screen smashed to bits.

I was mostly relieved I'd finally *have* to go buy a new one.

I headed off to AT&T. But when I went to pay, the formerly genial salesman suddenly exploded, "No! I just decided I can't sell this to you. I can't explain why, but you must go to Apple. Trust me." He seemed as befuddled as I was about why he was even saying this.

Now, logic would have said to be outraged, argue, whatever. But why bother?

So I went over to Apple, and just as I was about to charge $400, a saleswoman came running. She whispered fervently in my ear, "Girl, I could get fired for this, but do *not*, I repeat *not*, buy this phone here! The same one is on sale at Best Buy for a hundred and forty-nine dollars. Girl, you *hear* me?"

I hugged her and headed to Best Buy. Brava, Divine Source! You brought me a new phone for $250 less than I'd planned.

LIGHT LUGGAGE

This entire journey has been about getting lighter. Lightening the emotional burden you carry from the past. Lightening the clutter from your house. Lightening your private personal collection of resentments and vendettas. In fact, you're releasing *anything* that's blocked the Flow.

Once I was packing for a trip to Guanajuato and San Miguel de Allende, two of my favorite towns perched in the mountains of Mexico. While I'm not one of those who schleps two hair dryers and six pairs of shoes, I did have a normal-size suitcase with enough clothes for warm days, cold nights, and rain. Oh, and a few books.

Well, 10 minutes before my ride, I pulled the zipper to its final close, and the entire thing ripped to shreds. It was *done*.

There was an inevitable minute of "Are you freakin' *kidding me*? With no time to repack?" But then, because you recalibrate *fast* the more you offer, little time was wasted resisting. I offered the entire mess to Love. As I took a few deep breaths, a new thought rose over the horizon, *Wrong bag! Just take the teensy one.*

So I grabbed my carry-on, though I'd be traveling for two weeks. With no time to ponder, I asked God to take over my body and show what should come. My brain became quiet while my hands combed through stuff and just grabbed. Sweater, bathing suit, yoga stuff—item after item was flung into the bag. No books. Computer back under the bed.

The second I finished, my phone buzzed. The ride!

But here's what's interesting. First, I flew from San Francisco to L.A. to catch the leg to Mexico. And because there's an Eternal Divine Dictate that all flights into LAX must circle for at least 20 minutes before landing and then taxi for another 20 while they wonder why the hell there's no freakin' gate, we were *really* late. With only minutes to spare, I ran to the next terminal for Mexico, rolling the carry-on like a happy child. I wondered if people's checked bags would get there in time.

They did not.

Many hours later, I got dropped into the center of bustling Guanajuato, where I hadn't been in years. I'd planned on staying at a hotel that seemed like an amazing treehouse online. When I asked someone how to find it, she pointed straight up a tumble-down hill of colorful homes and giggled, "*¡Cuidate! ¡Trescientos escaleras!*"

Three. Hundred. Steps.

No problema. With the magic carry-on, this was just a morning workout. But I shuddered to think what would have occurred if I'd lugged the other bag.

Throughout the trip, I constantly marveled at how the Divine had *insisted* I not be burdened with heavy baggage. She'd known *ahead* of time all that was needed, and it was so much less than I'd ever guessed.

ꙅIVINE ORDER

You know by now that Divine Order is neither attached pursuit nor downtrodden passivity. You align with the highest outcome and let yourself be guided to the right actions at the right time. And sometimes with a specific problem, the correct route is simply to wait. You'll know when a door opens. If you trust that all needs will be answered, you'll *never* have to convince anyone, change their mind, or prove your worth. The situations and people in energetic harmony with you instinctively already know and arrive at the right time.

Divine Order? Wait. You mean that, intrinsically, the Divine is exquisitely patterned? You mean that it's not actually Divine Disarray that I'm doomed to be sweeping up after until the end of time? You mean that the emotional chaos I've attributed to Creation is just a wee bit of projection based on—among other things—the emotional chaos of not bonding with my parents? You mean that if I know something to be beautiful and good, then God does as well, and with a knowing that includes more love and perfection than I can comprehend?

Maybe this could work. Maybe I could invoke the optimal patterning that I know to exist and trust it to belong to Love as part of Divine Order. Maybe this is a kinder relationship than I'd ever imagined. Oh please, let this be true!

Gloriously guided by love

You may have noticed this yourself. After doing these practices for a while, the attachment to somber rule books about how to be spiritual falls away. You sense this extravagant power of grace and intelligence waiting to engage with you ever more deeply, sometimes in the most unexpected ways.

For me, you have really put the fun back into knowing the Divine. I remember God every moment now, the One I knew as a child. I remember sitting with this Love, being certain of my safety and my place. Now that feeling is back, and it's amazing, familiar, and too moving for words.

Thank for teaching me how to offer. There is such power in surrender. The moment I offer all back to God, a sweet sense of relief washes over me, regardless of whether "the answer" comes fast or slow.

Thank you for my new ability to let the answers come as they wish. And for telling stories of the funny ways things unfold . . . with God. This lets me move with ease and grace through difficult times!

Finally, thank you for reminding me that every day is not only a conversation with God, it's a love affair. I feel madly in love with It. And as I love, I am gloriously guided, protected, and carried through the days. All I must do is invite and open, which gets easier every day.

Because I was so ready to learn all of this, your work came.

So here's a prayer for opening to this Love.

Dear Lord, help me trust that there is a Plan far beyond what I can see through my veil of fears and illusions. May I move in harmony with Your Flow, knowing in every moment all needs will be met and You Alone guide me. Fill me with Your nourishing and extravagant Love. I am Yours, You are mine, we are One. All is well.

LAST-MINUTE DECISION

I have one final story for you. A few years ago, I was at the home of a friend as she hovered on the brink of death. For many months, she'd been slowly declining from colon cancer, and her friends and family had all gathered around.

This was a woman who'd been very accomplished by the standard yardsticks of our culture. She had two children she loved deeply. She'd made a great living as a celebrated costume designer and even won a couple Golden Globes for her work. She owned a cozy home in Marin

County, one of the loveliest parts of California, filled with exotic treasures from her trips around the world. She'd had a life many people might envy.

Well, if you've ever been at a deathbed, you know people can move into amazing clarity as they prepare to cross to the Other Side. That's what happened here. A kind of preternatural lucidity seemed to fill this woman, and as she spoke, I knew I was hearing a message I'd carry to my own last breath.

She said in a wavering, wistful voice, "I have only one huge regret—that I never gave my life to something beyond my daily desires. I had two great children and so many chances to be creative. But every step of the way, I only did what I thought would make me happy. I never once asked God, 'How can I serve *You*? I mean, really, how can I serve You?' Who knows what might have happened if I had?"

The skin on her face was so pale and drawn, it was almost transparent. Her son, who was sitting on the bed holding her hand, whispered urgently, "Mom, It's not too late! If you want to ask that, you still can." She smiled at him for a long time and closed her eyes.

The tangible peace and lightness that entered the room as she departed made me certain that she finally had.

And who knows how that may have affected, well . . . *everything.*

Final Meditation

Focus on your breath for a moment, breathing in calming energy and breathing out any worry or fear. As you breathe, feel yourself relaxing into a deep and quiet place inside, a place that's always been waiting for your return.

As you rest there, imagine one more time that all your finances are offered to this radiant Love. You can turn your hands to the sky and see all of it, every concern, every burden, every bill, offered back to Love. You can say, "You know my every need and now, finally, All is Yours. Let the Highest occur in every way."

Feel the peace and the release of that.

But take one more step. Imagine, now that the money has been fully offered, something else wants to be offered as well.

Your whole Being.

And you are ready.

You feel this all-knowing Force of Love has been waiting for You. It now fully accepts and rejoices in your sacred offering. Of yourself. All of you. Without any need to become more deserving.

Without any need to improve. You have been worthy to belong to Love all along.

In fact, You are Love Itself.

Love owns you now.

Relax and feel this for a few minutes.

Then open your eyes.

Resources for Going Deeper

This act of letting the Divine take the lead takes practice and commitment until it develops a life of its own. So here are some resources that can support you during this process. The first few are available on my website: ToshaSilver.com.

Resources from My Work

Living Outrageous Openness Forum. This online community started in 2015 to truly help people let the Divine take the lead. Included are weekly calls with me and a private Facebook group of people from around the world.

Classes. Several classes on the website give extensive additional information about topics in this book.

- Both Psychic Development and Psychic Development 2.0 (for help with cords and chakras)
- Shifting Desires into Preferences
- Balancing Giving and Receiving

- Offering: The Key to Joy
- Invite the Inner Kali Power

Full Abundance Change Me Prayer. If you enjoy using this prayer, you can easily get it on my website. There's a complimentary version to download and also a lovely high-resolution version to purchase that's suitable for framing.

Social Media. You can also find me almost every day on Instagram or my Facebook author page. I love sharing examples of the wild ways the Divine constantly intercedes when we finally begin to pay attention. Come join me!

OTHER RESOURCES

There are some good resources if you want to go deeper into the roots of the beautiful and ancient spiritual practices of offering and surrender.

- The *Yoga Sutras of Patanjali*
- Bhagavad Gita
- Any of the poetry of Rumi and Hafiz
- Florence Scovel Shinn's *The Game of Life and How to Play It*

Acknowledgments

One of my favorite sayings is that if God wants you to do something, She'll either give you the strength to do it or She'll bring the right help. I guess in this case, She did both. There are many people who saved my butt during the lengthy process of creating this book, and I apologize in advance if I've forgotten anyone.

First, my good friend and manager, Matt Klein, treated me with patience, kindness, and humor every day of this journey.

Stephanie Tade, my astonishing Buddhist-warrior agent, also was (and is) an amazing friend and supporter. I bow to her for listening with compassionate attention whenever I had a passing fit or two, and for making magic happen.

Gratitude to Patty Gift and Lisa Cheng for their thoughtful and courageous navigation of this complex process. Thank you, Anne Barthel, for arriving in the final hour to victoriously carry us across the finish line with eloquence and grace.

Melissa Lowenstein, the initial editor who knew how to brilliantly transform the transcripts of the original It's Not Your Money course into workable documents, was invaluable!

Kelly Malone (aka the Portuguese Dancing Queen) was the second editor who fine-tuned the entire piece to get it ready for submission. Without her Aries enthusiasm and humor, coupled with her remarkable skill for always knowing the right word at the right time, I'd never have been able to finish. She's become one of my most cherished friends.

Natalie Haggerty, my Snake Queen writing companion, did months and months of FaceTime study hall sessions with me. I honestly don't know what I would have done without her.

David Lane continued to be a source of hysterical inspiration and help, just as he was for all my previous books.

Bodi Regan, Hanna Weare, Sarah Buscho, and Sarah Drew have been enormous and faithful friends to me forever. Thank you.

Then there was the Calvary of healers who arrived to bring me back to health when I sustained serious injuries to both knees right in the middle of all this— Kerry Haworth, Matthew Graham, Andy Lesko, and Rodney McBride.

And thank you to the hundreds of gorgeous souls who signed up for the initial It's Not Your Money online course. Your enthusiastic encouragement helped make this a book.

Finally, a deep thank you to Shaun Herman Merkord . . . just because.

ABOUT THE AUTHOR

Tosha Silver graduated from Yale with a degree in English literature, but along the way fell madly in love with yogic philosophy. For the past 30 years she's taught people around the world ways to align with Inner Love. She's the author of *Outrageous Openness*, *Change Me Prayers*, and *Make Me Your Own*. She lives near San Francisco, where she runs an online school called Living Outrageous Openness, which offers ongoing support to those who follow these beautiful, ancient practices. Find out more at ToshaSilver.com.

Tosha particularly enjoys finding fresh, funny ways to embrace the Divine while avoiding conventional jargon and clichés at all cost. She loves how the sacred and mundane are truly One. Love Itself begins to lead when it is sincerely invited—by anyone.

The Universe is a Divine party.

Come as You are!

Hay House Titles of Related Interest

YOU CAN HEAL YOUR LIFE, the movie, starring Louise Hay & Friends
(available as an online streaming video)
www.hayhouse.com/louise-movie

THE SHIFT, the movie,
starring Dr. Wayne W. Dyer
(available as an online streaming video)
www.hayhouse.com/the-shift-movie

~

*CLAIM YOUR POWER: A 40-Day Journey to Discover, Live,
and Prosper in Your Life's True Purpose,* by Mastin Kipp

*EVERYTHING IS HERE TO HELP YOU: A Loving Guide to
Your Soul's Evolution,* by Matt Kahn

*THANK & GROW RICH: A 30-Day Experiment in Shameless
Gratitude and Unabashed Joy,* by Pam Grout

*WHAT IF THIS IS HEAVEN? How Our Cultural Myths Prevent Us
from Experiencing Heaven on Earth,* by Anita Moorjani

WORTHY: Boost Your Self-Worth to Grow Your Net Worth,
by Nancy Levin

All of the above are available at your local bookstore,
or may be ordered by contacting Hay House (see next page).

~

More guidance for abundance from
TOSHA SILVER

THE Wild Offering ORACLE

Let this beautifully illustrated card deck encourage you to experiment with Wild Offering: offering all to the Divine with complete and utter abandon. When you fully surrender and offer any topic to Spirit, you begin to release a tremendous burden. You no longer have to solve the problem from the ego. You immediately feel lighter and begin to get out of your own way. The right help and actions amazingly and spontaneously get shown at the right time.

Each card addresses a particular situation (Abundance, Ambition, Money, Solitude, Travel, Truth) with a comment or invocation that facilitates calling in Love for the highest outcome—even, sometimes, the miraculous.

www.hayhouse.com

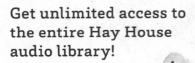